# ONE REP MAX:

## A GUIDE TO BEGINNING WEIGHT TRAINING

**Phillip A. Sienna, Ed.D.**
Mission College

Brown &
Benchmark

Library of Congress Cataloging Publication Data:

SIENNA, PHILLIP A., 1947-

ONE REP MAX: A GUIDE TO BEGINNING WEIGHT TRAINING




Cover Design: Gary Schmitt

Art: Craig Gosling, John Nixon, Ellen Traub


Library of Congress Catalog Card number: 88-70415

ISBN: 0-697-14826-2




Printed in the United States of America

10 9 8 7 6 5 4

The Publisher and Author disclaim responsibility for any adverse effects or consequences from the misapplication or injudicious use of the information contained within this text.

# DEDICATION

This book is dedicated with deep affection to Waino Fillback and the memory of Sebastian "Prof" Gallitto, two of my high school coaches who have had a significant influence on my life. Thank you both for making that commitment to work with young men and instill in them the values necessary to be successful in life. I consider myself very fortunate to have had the opportunity to play for both of you and to have been guided by your wisdom and knowledge.

# TABLE OF CONTENTS

# ACKNOWLEDGEMENTS

No work of this magnitude can be accomplished without the help of many people. First, I would like to thank Mark Macias and Anthony Ervin, students at Mission College, for posing for most of the exercises presented in this book. Second, I would like to thank the following organizations for graciously supplying pictures used throughout the text: The United States Weightlifting Federation; The National Strength Coaches Association, and *Power USA* magazine. Third, I would like to thank my wife, not only for her support and understanding throughout this project, but also for serving as a model for some of the exercises. And lastly, I would like to thank Craig Gosling and John Nixon, for doing an outstanding job with the illustrations; and the staff at Benchmark Press, particularly Becky Claxton for her keen editorial review and enthusiasm for the manuscript, and Butch Cooper, who believed in my ideas for this book and supported my efforts throughout the entire process.

# PREFACE TO INSTRUCTORS

I can remember sitting in my office several years ago, after receiving the 10th or 11th complimentary copy of a physical fitness book, thinking that if I received another one just like all of the others, I was going to scream. If you took away the covers, the information and formats were essentially indistinguishable between the books. Now that all of the publishers in our field have printed their fitness book, it appears that weight training is the new market area to be cloned and saturated.

I want to assure you that *ONE REP MAX* is not just another weight training book. This is the last thing that any of us need. It is truly with a strong conviction, the result of teaching weight training classes all of my professional career, that these classes could and should be taught differently that I undertook to write *ONE REP MAX* in the first place.

I realize that many instructors do not believe that a beginning weight training class is the appropriate time to introduce cognitive concepts and principles. It is their belief that such information should be reserved for an advanced level class. However, it has been my experience that advanced level classes primarily address advanced training routines, not advanced (nor beginning) training information. We also make the assumption that students will take a higher level weight training class, which is not always the situation. Consequently, we have many students who proceed through our programs without ever gaining an understanding of what is happening to them when they train with weights.

If you look at *ONE REP MAX*, you will see a lot of distinctions between it and other books that are presently on the market. The whole focus of the book is not on presenting information, but rather on having the students understand the information that is presented. Consequently, it has been my intent to create a book that has a writing style and delivery mode that is inviting and enjoyable for the students to read and comprehend.

Physiological concepts are presented in a way that should be understandable to most readers regardless of their background. The focus is on learning how a particular principle works, not on all of the intricate details involved in the process. There are retention sections interspersed throughout the chapters to ensure that the students are understanding the information that is being presented. If they do not respond appropriately to these questions, they can review the information before proceeding to another section in the chapter.

As you can see by revewing the Table of Contents, the book is certainly comprehensive. However, it is important to understand that comprehensive doesn't have to mean, or imply, complicated. Most of the chapters are short and concise and designed to aid student retention of the information that is presented.

There are many unique chapters in the book such as the Weakest Point Principle (Chapter 6); Nervous System Influence Over Muscle (Chapter 9); the breakdown of nutrition into two chapters, Energy Production (Chapter 11) and Muscle Growth (Chapter 12); Understanding Injuries (Chapter 15); Safety in the Weight Room (Chapter 16); and Weight Training Through the Years (Chapter 17). In addition, most of the other chapters have some information that is unique in terms of having the students understand how their bodies function.

A common complaint that we, in the physical education profession, receive from other disciplines is that our skill classes are not academic enough. If you look at the information presented in *ONE REP MAX*, it is obvious that this indictment does not have to be so. I am certainly not advocating that we abandon the skills part of a beginning weight training class. It is extremely important and an integral part of the course. I am saying, however, that the cognitive part of a weight training class is equally important and should also be addressed. Finding that balance for each of us as instructors is the real challenge. The intent of *ONE REP MAX* is to make that challenge a little easier for all of us to attain.

Phillip A. Sienna
Mission College

# PREFACE TO STUDENTS

Through all my years of teaching beginning weight training classes, I have never lost my fascination with and marvel at the human body. With all of its intricate checks and balances, I am always amazed at how efficient it is and how well it functions.

I have always tried to impart my fascination and respect for the human body to the students I have taught. There is so much that we take for granted and so much that we abuse, yet it appears that our bodies are very forgiving, especially when we are young, in trying to keep us on a even keel (called homeostasis).

I have presented a lot of information in *ONE REP MAX* that will help you gain a better understanding of how your body works and responds to resistive exercise (weight training). It has been my experience that students interested in weight training want to know as much as they can about the body. Hopefully, this book will address many of your questions and concerns about weight training and will make you more knowledgeable and confident in this area. Certainly, if you can absorb much of the information presented in *ONE REP MAX*, I can assure you that you will have an outstanding grasp of many key areas and issues in weight training.

It has been my intent to make the book inviting for you to read. I didn't just throw out principles and concepts but tried to explain them in a way that will make sense to you. In most chapters, there are retention sections that will help you determine if you are comprehending the information that has been presented. If you are not answering the questions appropriately, you can go back to those sections to review the information. Also, there are many unique chapters to this book that will help fill in the gaps concerning your complete understanding of weight training.

There really isn't any mystery to training with weights. By knowing the guidelines and applying the principles, the adaptations that the body makes are fairly predictable. Often times, we tend to rely on other people's opinions and judgements when, with the proper information, we could be making those decisions for ourselves. By taking the time to learn the information presented in *ONE REP MAX*, you can make yourself into a more knowledgeable, confident, and independent consumer. It is my hope that this book can help you attain that objective.

Phillip A. Sienna
Mission College

# 1

# Introduction to Weight Training

Weight training has become an extremely popular activity in recent years. Although much of this popularity can be attributed to several factors such as an increase in athletic participation, the greatest contribution has come from the public and its awareness of the need for a physically fit body. Although people train with weights for a variety of reasons, it is more acceptable today to use weights simply to enhance one's appearance by firming up muscle tissue and reducing body fat.

## WEIGHT TRAINING IN SPORT

It is interesting to note the rapid advancement that weight training has received in the athletic community over the past few decades. In the 1950s and early 1960s, many coaches in strength-dominated sports such as football did not want their athletes to lift weights because they feared that it would make them muscle bound and impair their performance. It was not until the 1980s, that coaches of finesse sports such as tennis, golf, baseball, and basketball would allow their athletes near a weight room. They believed that weight training would ruin their athletes "touch." Both of these original perceptions (muscle boundness and loss of touch) have subsequently been dispelled as athletes have demonstrated in all sports that improving their strength has been a major factor in their improved performances. This relationship of the improvement in strength to athletic success has been so strong and consistent over the years that most professional and major college athletic departments now employ full-time weight training coaches whose primary responsibility is to improve the strength and power of their respective athletes (Figure 1.1).

The sport of body building also has contributed to the growing interest in weight training. A significant influence has come from Arnold Schwarzenegger (former amateur and professional body building champion), whose success in the entertainment industry has done much to focus the public's attention on the sport of building body. There are now more local body building contests as well as more amateur and professional athletes participating in the sport (Figure 1.2). Whether you find the body builder's physique particularly attractive or not, objectively it is hard to deny the amazing muscle development that these athletes are able to obtain from their training.

As stated earlier, the biggest participatory advancement in weight training has occurred with the recreational athlete. Where previously only competitive athletes lifted weights to prepare for their sport, it is acceptable today for anyone wanting to get in good physical condition to train with weights. This increased desire on the part of the public to utilize weights has led to an unprecedented expansion of weight training facilities and health clubs during the past two decades.

**Figure 1.1.** *A spacious and immaculately clean college weight room. Some of the more successful collegiate programs spare no expense when it comes to purchasing strength equipment for their athletes. (Courtesy of the National Strength Coaches Association)*

Weight training has developed into a massive industry with plenty of competitors vying for your interests (money). Unfortunately, there is some misleading information concerning various aspects of weight training. Body builders in particular seem more prone to participate in some of these dubious practices, in an attempt to develop massive muscle size and definition. Regrettably, some of these unscientific practices filter down to recreational athletes who may, in turn, experiment with them to see if they work. Also, many health clubs, in an attempt to boost membership, make somewhat inflated and unsubstantiated claims about the benefits of their gym and equipment. Therefore, it is

**Figure 1.2.** *An amateur Mr. Muscle Beach contest drew some quality competitors in the small, northern California coastal town of Santa Cruz.*

imperative to protect yourself from much of this misinformation concerning strength development by becoming a knowledgeable and discriminating consumer. The concepts and principles presented in this book will help you determine fact from fallacy and recognize misleading practices and inaccurate information.

## BENEFITS OF WEIGHT TRAINING

### Strength/Hypertrophy

The most obvious benefit from a weight training program is that your muscles will become stronger and somewhat larger, depending upon your sex, genetic background and the type of routine that you use (Figure 1.3). Women do not obtain as much muscle hypertrophy (enlargement) from their training programs as men; yet, they realize significant increases in strength. This should be reassuring to many women who are fearful of obtaining large, male-like physiques.

### Tone/Posture/Rehabilitation

Muscle will become tighter from a weight training program; consequently, when in a relaxed state, it will not appear soft or flaccid. This is referred to as muscle tone. Weight training also can help improve poor posture by strengthening muscles that have becomed

**Figure 1.3.** *One of weight training's obvious benefits for males in an increase in muscle size. Women have a much more difficult time increasing muscle size, which is something that they may not desire. Here, an amateur body builder shows outstanding muscle development and definition.*

stretched and weakened, thereby aligning body parts more advantageously. In addition, weight training is used in the rehabilitative process of an injured muscle or joint to assist in getting it back to its normal function.

### Metabolism

Because muscle tissue is metabolically active at rest, (it burns calories in this state; fat does not), having more muscle tissue will somewhat ensure that your basal metabolic rate (rate at which you burn calories in a resting state) will remain high as you age. It has been well-substantiated that a certain percentage of muscle tissue is lost as one ages (approximately 3 to 5 percent every 10 years after the age of 25). Also, there is less energy needed for growth, which results in a further decrease in metabolism. However, most adults do not decrease their appetites to match this decrease in metabolism; consequently, it is easy to see how the average middle-aged American can get fatter with age. A weight training program can help minimize the decrease in muscle tissue with age and ensure the burning of more calories at rest and a lesser chance of obesity.

## Flexibility/Stability

Contrary to what many people may believe, weight training has the potential to increase one's flexibility if the exercises are performed correctly. It is important to do each exercise with a full range of motion (ROM), which will ensure that the muscle is being fully stretched as well as contracted. Weight training also has the ability to increase joint stability since it strengthens ligaments and tendons as well as muscle.

## Endurance

By increasing strength from a weight training program, it also is possible to increase muscle endurance. Since you are raising your peak strength value, any weight under that should feel lighter and you should be able to do more repetitions. Consequently, lifting objects should be easier and you shouldn't feel as fatigued in pursuing your daily endeavors.

## Psychological

In addition to the obvious physiological benefits of weight training, there are some definite psychological ones as well. Physically looking the best that you can has the potential to enhance self-esteem. People who train with weights like the tight feeling that accompanies the exercising of their muscles. It is an indication that they are doing something healthy for their body. In addition, weight training is a good outlet for relieving frustration and tension. The long-term adaptations that the body makes in response to the training program positively reinforces the effort for many people. For example, improved strength and endurance, reduction in unsightly body fat and an increase in toned and defined muscles all contribute to the psychological benefits of training with weights. If you look and feel better about yourself physically, there is a strong correlation that you will look and feel better about yourself psychologically as well.

# 2

# Key Training Principles

As with any sport, there are certain principles you should know and understand in weight training in order to maximize the results and benefits you derive from your training program. By following three key training principles, you are more likely to obtain these desired results. Unfamiliarity with these principles could possibly result in disappointment and frustration since the body will not respond in an appropriate manner (increased strength, endurance, tone or hypertrophy) unless it is exercised or stressed properly.

The following three principles, tension, overload, and specificity, are the key ones to comprehend in terms of gaining a basic understanding of weight training. It is important to become familiar with these principles since the benefits that occur from any training program are the direct result of the application of these principles.

## TENSION PRINCIPLE

The key to developing strength is simply creating tension in a muscle. Generally, the greater the tension created in a muscle, the greater the strength gains. The most traditional and still most common way to create tension in a muscle is by using weights. However, it is important to realize that anything that creates tension in a muscle, whether it is caused by using weights, machines, elastic or rubber bands, or immovable objects, will result in greater strength.

Anytime you contract your muscles, you are creating tension in them. Mild contractions will result in mild tension being produced in the muscle, which will ultimately lead to small gains in strength. Stronger contractions will result in greater tension being produced in the muscle, which will lead to greater gains in strength. If you want to significantly increase strength, you will have to find a way to create more tension in your muscles. The easiest way to accomplish this in the weight room is to simply use heavier resistances. The heavier the resistances or weights used, the greater the tension that is produced in the muscle. Using light weights in an attempt to get stronger will compromise your strength potential since you are not creating a lot of tension in your muscles.

It is important to understand that it really does not matter what type of equipment you use to create tension in your muscles. Although many equipment manufacturers would like to convince you otherwise, the type of equipment is really subordinate to the principle of creating tension. As long as you are creating tension, have confidence that your muscles will become stronger. What matters most is the *quality* of your workout, not the equipment or facility.

## OVERLOAD PRINCIPLE

The overload principle is the basis for increasing or improving strength. Figure 2.1 illustrates how the overload principle works to improve strength. Every person starts out with an initial level of strength. Once an overload is applied (traditionally in the form of weights) and the muscle adapts to that resistance, or stress, a new or higher level of strength is attained. Additional overloads (increasing resistance) will result in still greater gains in strength.

As long as an individual continues to overload, the adaptation to that stress on the muscle will be an increase in strength. However, once a desired level of strength is attained, no further overload is necessary. The individual can then begin a maintenance program designed to hold onto the strength gains that have been attained.

Muscle tissue has the ability to react to physical stresses placed upon it (in this case, represented by an overload in weight training) in one of three ways. As you can see from Figure 2.2, if an overload on the muscle is adequate, an increase in strength will occur. If the overload is too great, however, muscle will respond by either breaking down (an injury) or by a decrease in performance (loss of strength). If the overload is inadequate, there will be no adaptation by the muscle and nothing will happen (no increase in strength).

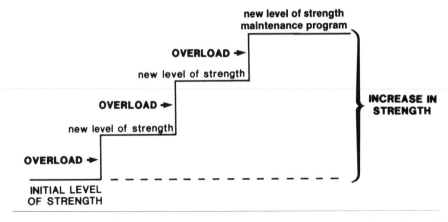

**Figure 2.1.** *An illustration of how the overload principle contributes to an increase in strength. Notice that once the muscle has adapted to the original overload, a new overload must be placed on the muscle for subsequent-gains in strength to occur.*

---

Underload → No increase in strength
Proper overload → Increase in strength
Too great an overload → Loss of strength, fatigue, injury

---

**Figure 2.2.** *The consequences of too little, just the right amount, and too much overload on the muscle.*

## Ways to Overload

Figure 2.3 illustrates several ways to apply an overload in the weight room. Any of these methods of overloading will produce an increase in muscle strength, endurance, tone, definition or hypertrophy. If you wish to significantly increase strength or muscle size (hypertrophy), overloading with weight, sets or days would be more effective than overloading with repetitions or decreasing the recovery time in between sets. The latter two ways are more appropriate for enhancing muscle endurance rather than muscle strength. Any time that you do more repetitions, you have to use a lighter resistance. Decreasing the recovery time in between sets also forces you to use lighter weights since your muscles will not be fully recovered from the last set. Remember, if you are creating less tension in your muscles because you are using lighter resistances, your improvement in strength will, in all probability, be minimized.

---

### METHODS OF OVERLOADING
1. Increase weight (s)
2. Increase repetitions (e)
3. Increase sets (s)
4. Increase exercises (s)
5. Increase number of workouts (s)
6. Decrease recovery time between sets (e)

---

**Figure 2.3.** *Ways to apply an overload to the muscles. The e or s in parentheses primarily indicates whether the overload benefits strength or endurance.*

## SPECIFICITY PRINCIPLE

The specificity principle refers to the fact that the body will respond or adapt in a very specific manner to the type of demands or training that you place upon it. By placing a specific demand on the body, you get a specific response or adaptation (see Figure 2.4). If you engage in aerobic exercise (specific demand), the specific adaptation by the body will be a stronger heart and cardiovascular system. If you train anaerobically by doing wind sprints (specific demand), the specific adaptation from that training will be an increase in running speed. In the same respect, if you want to develop strength, you need to train in a very specific manner (specific demand) to obtain that very specific response.

Recalling the tension principle, it is obvious that to develop strength, you have to lift heavy weights with few repetitions. If you do otherwise (lifted light weights with many repetitions), you would be demanding something very different from your muscles (muscle endurance). Increasing your ability to do repeated contractions (muscle endurance) will do little to significantly improve strength. Therefore, it is extremely important that you understand this principle and realize how the body is going to respond or adapt to the type of demand or training that you place upon it in the weight room. It is unrealistic to expect an increase in strength when you are using light weights and many repetitions in

## SPECIFICITY PRINCIPLE

| Demand on Body | | Adaptation by Body |
|---|---|---|
| Inactivity | = | Loss of strength, definition, size |
| Aerobic exercise (Jogging, etc.) | = | Stronger heart, cardiovascular system, better endurance |
| Anaerobic exercise (Sprinting) | = | Sprint faster |
| Heavy weight training | = | Increase in muscle strength, size |
| Light weight training | = | Increase in muscle endurance |

**Figure 2.4.** *The response of the body to various specific physical demands placed upon it. Notice that to get a specific response, you have to train the body in a very specific way.*

your training. You can't expect the body to do something (increase strength) that it hasn't been prepared to do. Remember that weight training involves the training of your muscles to develop greater strength, larger mass, greater definition (tone) or better endurance. To get that type of specific result (adaptation) from your program takes a very specific type of training routine (demand).

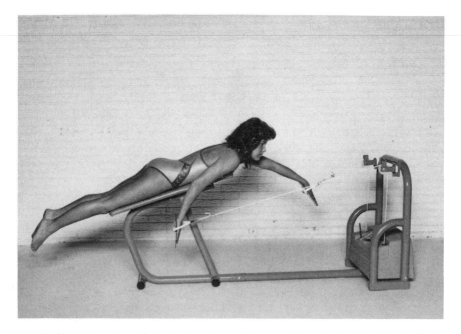

**Figure 2.5.** *Weight-training equipment designed to strengthen specific movements in swimming. A-swim bench. Courtesy of Fitness Systems, Inc., Independence, MO.*

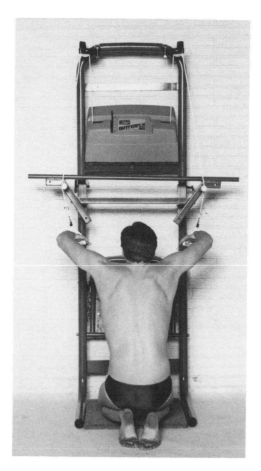

**Figure 2.5.** *(continued) B-butterfly station.*

---

The key to developing strength is simply creating _____ in a muscle.

TENSION

The greater the amount of tension created in a muscle, the _____ (GREATER, LESSER) the gains in strength that will occur.

GREATER

The easiest way to create greater tension in a muscle in a weight room is to simply use _____ (HEAVIER, LIGHTER) weights.

HEAVIER

Lifting lighter weights and many repetitions _____ (WILL, WILL NOT) produce significantly greater gains in strength.

WILL NOT

It _____ (DOES, DOES NOT) matter what type of equipment that you work out on as long as you can create tension in your muscles.

DOES NOT

By gradually increasing the resistance that you work out with, you are applying which principle in weight training? (TENSION, OVERLOAD, SPECIFICITY)

OVERLOAD

If you overload too much or too quickly in the weight room, you may have either a decrease in performance (strength), or be _____.

INJURED

Not overloading enough will result in _____ (NO GAIN IN STRENGTH, GAIN IN STRENGTH, GAIN IN ENDURANCE).

NO GAIN IN STRENGTH

Which is the best overload method to use, of the three choices given, to increase strength? (INCREASE WEIGHT, INCREASE REPETITIONS, DECREASE RECOVERY TIME)

INCREASE WEIGHT

Overloading by increasing the number of repetitions will increase _____ (STRENGTH, ENDURANCE).

ENDURANCE

Increasing the number of sets done for an exercise or muscle group will increase _____ (STRENGTH, ENDURANCE).

STRENGTH

The specificity principle states that the body will respond or adapt in a very _____ manner or way to the type of demands placed upon it.

SPECIFIC

The specificity principle implies that it _____ (IS, IS NOT) possible to significantly increase strength by lifting light weights and doing many repetitions.

IS NOT

According to the specificity principle, you have to train the body in a specific way (demand) to have it respond in a specific _____ (adaptation).

MANNER

# 3

# Definitions

Every sport has its own vocabulary. With weight training, there are a few terms that need to be defined so when referring to them throughout the text you have a clear picture of what they mean.

## STRENGTH

In the context of weight training, strength is defined as the ability of a muscle to exert force. Maximum strength is the ability of a muscle to exert maximum force. It is measured or determined in the weight room by the maximal amount of weight that can be lifted one time. This is referred to as one repetition maximum, or ONE REP MAX, and abbreviated as 1-RM. Any time that you perform more than one repetition in determining strength, you also are determining, to some extent, muscle endurance. Max strength can only be determined by how much weight can be lifted in 1-RM.

## ENDURANCE

Endurance involves the ability of a muscle to do repeated contractions without fatigue. It is measured or determined in the weight room by taking either a percentage of a person's body weight, or max strength value, then doing as many repetitions as possible (Figure 3.1). The more reps completed, the greater the demonstration of muscle endurance. It is inherently more fair to use a certain percentage of the individual's 1-RM rather than body weight for an endurance test since each person would be working within his strength potential. It is not inconceivable that when using a certain percentage of body weight, an overweight individual may not have the strength to do even one repetition.

### Relationship of Strength to Endurance

It is interesting to note that improving strength will also improve muscle endurance if the weight remains the same for the two endurance tests. Referring to Figure 3.2, you can see that a 50-pound weight represents 50 percent of the max strength value (100 pounds) of the individual prior to a training program. With training, the individual improved his strength to 150 pounds, so that the 50 pounds now represents only 33 percent of his max strength value. The individual should be able to complete more repetitions since what he is lifting represents a lesser percent of his maximum strength potential.

### Progressive Resistive Exercise

This term is traditionally used in reference to weight training. The term "progressive" refers to the fact that the resistance should be applied in a gradual or progressive

## ASSESSING MUSCLE ENDURANCE

*Method #1—Percentage of Body Weight*
Body weight × percent     → Weight to be lifted  → Number of reps completed
Example: 200 lbs × 70%    → 140 lbs         → 7 reps completed

*Method #2—Percentage of One Rep Max*
One Rep Max × percent     → Weight to be lifted  → Number of reps completed
Example: 1-RM = 150 lbs. × 70%  → 105 lbs.      → 13 reps completed

**Figure 3.1.** *Two different methods for testing muscle endurance. Both involve taking a certain percentage of either a person's body weight or 1-RM.*

## RELATIONSHIP OF STRENGTH TO ENDURANCE

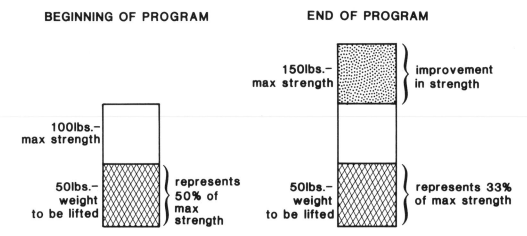

**Figure 3.2.** *An illustration showing how improving strength can improve muscle endurance when the resistance remains the same for the two tests.*

manner (overload concept). Although it is not as frequently used today, whenever you hear anything about resistive exercise, it is usually meant to refer to weight training or a similar type of activity.

## WORK

Work is simply defined as force times distance. For example, if someone lifts a 100-pound weight (applies a force) over a distance of two feet, then he has done 200-foot pounds of work (Figure 3.3). It is obvious from this definition that by increasing the ability of your muscles to generate force by improving your strength, you should be able

$$\text{Work} = \text{Force} \times \text{Distance}$$
$$\text{(Strength)}$$

Example:
$$\text{Work} = 100 \text{ lbs.} \times 2 \text{ feet}$$
$$\text{(Strength)}$$

$$\text{Work} = 200 \text{ foot pounds}$$

**Figure 3.3.** *The definition of work and an example of how it is calculated.*

to improve upon your ability to do more work. Generally, the more work you are able to accomplish in the weight room, the greater the improvement you can expect from your weight training program.

## POWER

Power is a concept that involves work; but it also involves another element that distinguishes it from work. Power is the rate of applying force, or doing work. Therefore, it involves work (force times distance), but also brings in the element of time or speed (Figure 3.4). For example, if two people can lift 100 pounds a distance of two feet then they both have done 200-foot pounds of work. From this example, you cannot conclude that either one was stronger than the other because they both did the same amount of work. However, if one of the individuals did the work in four seconds and the other in two seconds, it is fair to say that the second person is twice as powerful since he was able to apply the force in half the time (Figure 3.5). The second person is able to exert twice as much force in terms of foot pounds per second than the first person (100 compared with 50).

$$\text{Power} = \frac{\text{Work}}{\text{Time}} = \frac{\text{Force (Strength)} \times \text{Distance}}{\text{Time (Speed)}}$$

$$\text{Power} = \frac{200 \text{ foot pounds}}{4 \text{ seconds}}$$

$$\text{Power} = 50 \text{ foot pounds/second}$$

**Figure 3.4.** *The definition of power and an example of how it is calculated.*

## HOW RATE OF DOING WORK (APPLYING FORCE) AFFECTS POWER

Subject A

$$\text{Power} = \frac{\text{Work}}{\text{Time}}$$

$$\text{Power} = \frac{200 \text{ foot pounds}}{4 \text{ seconds}}$$

Power = 50 foot pounds/second

Subject B

$$\text{Power} = \frac{\text{Work}}{\text{Time}}$$

$$\text{Power} = \frac{200 \text{ foot pounds}}{2 \text{ seconds}}$$

Power = 100 foot pounds/second

**Figure 3.5.** *A comparison of how speed (time) affects power. The individual who is able to apply or exert force in a shorter period of time is more powerful.*

### Improving Power

It is possible to improve power by working on either speed (time) or strength (force). As you can see from Figure 3.6, an improvement in either one or both of these variables will result in an improvement in overall power. However, since improvement in speed is (1) limited by genetics, (2) increases very little, and (3) peaks rather quickly, an individual usually can benefit more by concentrating on improving strength rather than speed. Besides the fact that we do not come anywhere close to maximizing our true strength potential, increases in strength come in much greater dimensions and much more easily than increases in speed.

### SET

A set in weight training can be composed of any number of repetitions depending upon when the lifter becomes fatigued. For example, if an individual picked up a weight and completed 10 repetitions before putting the weight down, that would constitute one set of 10 repetitions. If the individual was to do another set of 10 repetitions, that would now constitute two sets of 10 repetitions. In weight training, routines are written out such that 3 × 8 would be interpreted as telling the lifter they are supposed to do three sets of eight repetitions. (Of course, the exercise and the amount of weight to be lifted would also be specified.) Doing more than one set of an exercise is one way to overload in weight training. Up to a point, the more sets that you complete, the greater the overload and subsequent gains in strength and hypertrophy that will occur.

# WAYS TO IMPROVE POWER

1. Increase force by increasing strength

2. Decrease time by increasing speed

3. Combination of increasing strength and speed

$$\text{POWER} = \frac{200 \text{ foot pounds}}{4 \text{ seconds}} = 50 \text{ foot pounds/second}$$

$$\begin{array}{c}\text{INCREASE FORCE} \\ \text{(STRENGTH)}\end{array} = \frac{300 \text{ foot pounds}}{4 \text{ seconds}} = 75 \text{ foot pounds/second}$$

$$\begin{array}{c}\text{INCREASE BOTH} \\ \text{FORCE (STRENGTH)} \\ \text{AND SPEED}\end{array} = \frac{300 \text{ foot pounds}}{3 \text{ seconds}} = 100 \text{ foot pounds/second}$$

**Figure 3.6.** *An example of how increasing force (strength), increasing speed (decreasing time) or a combination of both factors influences power.*

_____ (STRENGTH, ENDURANCE) is defined as the ability of the muscle to exert force.

STRENGTH

Maximal strength is measured in the weight room by determining how much weight can be lifted _____ (ONE, MORE THAN ONE) time.

ONE

One repetition maximum, or 1-RM, is an indication of muscle _____ (STRENGTH, ENDURANCE).

STRENGTH

The ability to do repeated contractions without fatigue is the definition for muscle _____ (STRENGTH, ENDURANCE).

ENDURANCE

If you selected a submaximal weight based on a certain percentage of a person's body weight or max strength value and then had him do as many repetitions as possible, that would be a test for muscle _____ (STRENGTH, ENDURANCE).

ENDURANCE

Which type of endurance test would be more fair to the heavier individual: one based on taking a certain percentage of body weight to determine the poundage to be lifted, or one based on his max strength value?

## MAX STRENGTH VALUE

Lifting heavier weights and few repetitions would be a good routine to improve muscle_____ (STRENGTH, ENDURANCE)?

## STRENGTH

Lifting lighter weights many times (15 or more reps) would be a good routine to develop muscle _____ (STRENGTH, ENDURANCE)?

## ENDURANCE

If the weight remains the same, then improving muscle strength _____ (WILL, WILL NOT) improve muscle endurance (the ability to do more repetitions using that weight).

## WILL

The term progressive resistive exercise traditionally has been used when referring to _____ .

## WEIGHT TRAINING

Progressive simply means that you increase the resistance in a _____ manner.

## GRADUAL

Force times distance is the definition of _____ (WORK, POWER, STRENGTH).

## WORK

One way to increase the force that you can exert and, consequently, the work that you can do is to improve your _____ (STRENGTH, ENDURANCE, POWER)?

## STRENGTH

Power involves work but also introduces the element of _____ ?

## TIME or SPEED

It is easier to improve power by working on STRENGTH (FORCE) or SPEED (TIME).

## STRENGTH (FORCE)

A _____ in weight training can consist of any number of repetitions.

## SET

A routine that indicated 2 × 12 would mean that the individual was to do 2 _____ (SETS, REPETITIONS) of 12 _____ (SETS, REPETITIONS).

## SETS, REPETITIONS

---

# 4

# Categories of Weightlifters

For clarification purposes, it is helpful to understand the differences between the various categories of weightlifters and weight trainers. Sometimes the terminology is applied incorrectly, causing confusion. A weight trainer is anyone who trains with weights. So, essentially, all recreational lifters, as well as competitive lifters, are weight trainers. Weightlifters, on the other hand, are athletes who use weights competitively. Under this category of weightlifter, you have the three classifications listed in Figure 4.1.

## OLYMPIC LIFTERS

Olympic lifting consists of two lifts: the clean and jerk and the snatch. The clean part of the clean and jerk involves taking the bar from the floor and lifting it to chest height (Figure 4.2). The second part of the movement (the jerk) involves extending the arms over head while doing a split with the legs (Figure 4.3). The snatch involves taking the bar from the floor to an overhead position in one movement (Figure 4.4). It is the combined total of weight lifted that determines the winner in each of the 10 weight categories. The most successful Olympic lifters come from the eastern bloc countries of Bulgaria, Rumania, East Germany and the Soviet Union. Olympic lifting has never been very popular in this country even though it is the only type of competitive lifting allowed in the Olympics.

Agility, flexibility and technique are extremely important factors in Olympic lifting. Strength alone cannot compensate for poor body mechanics or improper form. As you

---

### COMPETITIVE WEIGHTLIFTERS

Olympic —Clean and jerk
Snatch

Power —Bench press
Squat
Dead lift

Body Builder—Judge physique

---

**Figure 4.1.** *Classification of competitive weight lifters. Notice that body builders do not lift any weights during their competition but are judged only on the development of their physiques.*

**Figure 4.2.** *The clean part of the Olympic lift called the clean and jerk. Whenever you take a weight from the floor and bring it to your chest in the standing position, it is referred to as a clean. Notice the deep squat position the lifter assumes before standing up. Courtesy of the United States Weightlifting Federation (Bruce Klemens photo).*

**Figure 4.3.** *The jerk part of the Olympic lift called the clean and jerk. The jerk involves taking the bar from a clean position to an overhead position while jumping or splitting the legs to assist this movement. Courtesy of the United States Weightlifting Federation (Bruce Klemens photo).*

**Figure 4.4.** *The sequence of the snatch, the second Olympic lift. The snatch involves taking the bar from the floor to an overhead position in one motion. This lift requires a tremendous amount of shoulder girdle strength and flexibility. Courtesy of the United States Weightlifting Federation (Bruce Klemens photo).*

**Figure 4.5.** *In both the clean and jerk and the snatch, the lifter tries to lift the bar as high off the floor as possible before dropping underneath it. This maneuver takes a tremendous amount of skill, agility and quickness in addition to total body strength. This sequence is part of a clean prior to standing erect. Courtesy of the United States Weightlifting Federation (Bruce Klemens photo).*

can see in Figure 4.5, the athlete is not able to lift the bar that far off the platform. Consequently, he has to drop very quickly under the bar while trying to lift it as high as possible. If he cannot get his body underneath the bar, he will not be able to control the weight and will end up failing in his attempt. Notice the extremely awkward position (squat) that is the result of the lifter dropping underneath the bar. It takes a tremendous amount of leg and buttock strength to rise to the standing (clean) position.

## POWERLIFTERS

Power lifting involves three lifts: the bench press, the squat and the dead lift (Figure 4.6). In contrast to Olympic lifting where technique, agility and flexibility are extremely important, power lifting involves almost 100 percent brute strength. In power lifting, since speed is not a factor in completing a good lift, strength, rather than power, is the key element. As long as the weight is moving upward in a slow and steady fashion, the lifter will be given the green light signifying a good lift. Just as it is with Olympic lifting, the combined total weight lifted determines the winner in each weight category. Power lifting competitions are primarily held in the United States and European countries. Many countries (Eastern Bloc in particular) refuse to accept the sport of power lifting since it is not a recognized event in the Olympics.

## BODY BUILDERS

Body builders is the third type of competitive weightlifter. Unlike the first two categories of weightlifters, body builders do not lift any weights during competition. They are judged on how well they have developed their physiques (Figure 4.7). Judges are primarily looking for three things: muscle size, symmetry and definition. The athlete must possess exceptional development in all three areas to be successful.

The body builder, in order to be competitive, must develop some degree of stage presence. He has to learn how to present his physique in a way that accentuates his strong points and minimizes his weaknesses. The science of training in the gym is transformed into a performing art when he takes the stage (Figure 4.8). Confidence and charisma are important factors in convincing the judges that he is a champion. Those athletes who may have great muscle development but do not have this stage presence are usually not as successful as someone who is comfortable in front of people and loves to perform. Consequently, body builders must spend a great deal of time posing as well as training in order to learn how to present their development in the best manner possible.

The body builder's training is much different from that of Olympic lifters or powerlifters. Olympic and powerlifters are primarily concerned with strength (and technique for Olympic lifters) and train very specifically to develop that quality. The body builder is primarily concerned with muscle size, which requires a slightly different emphasis to his training program. Although body builders are very strong and lift heavy weights, they have to do many different exercises and sets working the same muscle group to ensure that it will develop properly.

Most of the time, body builders do not look like the pictures you see in magazines. During a good part of the year, they try to bulk up and put on as much muscle as possible. Anywhere from a month to three months prior to their competition, they go on a diet (sometimes severe) to try to reduce body fat. Athletes that haven't dieted properly will

**Figure 4.6.** *The three lifts involved in powerlifting competition: (a) the bench press, (b) the squat, and (c) the dead lift. Courtesy of Powerlifting USA Magazine.*

**Figure 4.7.** *The body builder concentrates on developing muscle size, symmetry and definition. Developing strength is a concern to the body builder only in terms of its importance in stimulating the muscle to increase in size (hypertrophy).*

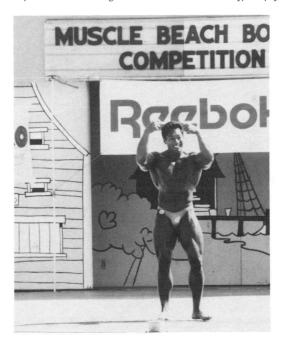

**Figure 4.8.** *The body builder has to learn how to present his physique in the best manner possible in order to be successful. Stage presence, which includes confidence and charisma, goes a long way in convincing the judges and spectators that you have what it takes to be a champion. Notice how this competitor projects his enjoyment of being in the spotlight.*

have muscles that look soft and undefined rather than "ripped." After competition, they try to bulk up again to gain larger muscles.

Body building is a real challenge in that the athlete must come to know his system and what works best for him in terms of developing his physique. Nowadays, most body builders try to stay fairly close to their competing weight so they do not have to go on protracted diets. This is much easier psychologically and physiologically as it tends to eliminate the yo-yo effect of extreme weight gain and loss.

It takes many years to develop into a top-notch body builder. With each competition, the athlete gains more information and feedback on how to better prepare for the next contest. It is somewhat of a trial and error approach: use what works best for you and discard the rest. Over the years of competition, then, they get a better idea of how to prepare for each contest as they continue to refine and define their physiques.

---

Individuals lifting weights for recreation are considered weight _____ (LIFTERS, TRAINERS).

TRAINERS

Identify the three types of competitive weightlifters.

OLYMPIC, POWER, BODY BUILDERS

Which type of competitive lifting requires the greatest amount of technique?

OLYMPIC LIFTING

Which type of competitive lifting requires the greatest amount of flexibility?

OLYMPIC LIFTING

Which type of lifting involves the snatch and clean and jerk?

OLYMPIC LIFTING

What are the three lifts that make up power lifting?

BENCH PRESS, SQUAT, DEAD LIFT

What type of lifting involves primarily pure strength, Olympic or power?

POWER LIFTING

Body builders for the most part _____ (ARE, ARE NOT) very strong.

ARE

For which type of lifter is dieting an integral part of his training?

BODY BUILDER

Which type of lifter has to do a lot of different exercises working the same muscle group for his training?

BODY BUILDER

---

# 5

# Types of Resistances

In Chapter 1, you learned that the key to increasing strength was to create tension in the muscle. The greater the tension created in the muscle, the greater the strength gains that will be developed. Tension is created in the muscle when it is forced to overcome a resistance. Traditionally, the equipment used to create this resistance has been weights and dumbbells. However, a muscle will respond to any type of tension generated in it, regardless of the source, by becoming stronger and larger. This tension could be applied to the muscle with weights or dumbbells, elastic or surgical tubing, machines, a person's own body weight or immovable objects. The type of resistance used is secondary to the ability to create tension in the muscle. As long as tension is created in the muscle, it will respond over a period of time by becoming stronger.

There are three type of resistances that can be applied to a muscle to produce tension: (1) fixed or constant, (2) variable, and (3) accommodating. Before discussing each type of resistance, however, it will be helpful to understand the concept of electromyography and how it is used in weight training to determine the effectiveness of the various types of resistances.

Most people are familiar with an electrocardiogram or what is commonly referred to as an EKG. An EKG recording measures the electrical output of the heart through surface electrodes placed on the chest cavity. In addition to the heart, there are other areas of the body that also produce their own electrical activity. For example, an electroencephalogram, or an EEG recording, measures electrical activity in the brain and an electromyogram, or an EMG recording, measures electrical activity in the muscle. It takes an electrical stimulus from the nervous system for muscle to contract. By placing electrodes on the surface of the muscle when it contracts, that electrical activity can be monitored and recorded.

As you can see from the simulated EMG recording in Figure 5.1, there is much more electrical activity occurring in the muscle when it contracts to overcome the 60 pounds of resistance. This is reflected in the magnitude of the recording on the graph. The harder or more forcefully a muscle contracts, the greater the electrical activity that will show up on the EMG recording.

---

The greater the tension generated in a muscle the _____ (GREATER, LESSER) the gains in strength that will occur.

GREATER

Tension is generated in a muscle by having it overcome a _____ .

RESISTANCE

Identify the three types of resistances.

FIXED, VARIABLE, ACCOMMODATING

An electromyogram, or EMG, records the _____ activity produced in the muscle when it contracts.

ELECTRICAL

More electrical activity recorded on the EMG is an indication of _____ (GREATER, LESSER) tension generated in the muscle.

GREATER

A 60-pound resistance when compared to a 20-pound resistance will cause greater _____ to be generated in the muscle when it contracts.

TENSION

---

## EMG RECORDINGS OF A BICEP CURL

**20lbs. resistance**          **60lbs. resistance**

**Figure 5.1.** *Simulated EMG recording from lifting a 20-pound and 60-pound weight.*

## FIXED (CONSTANT) RESISTANCE

Figure 5.2 shows a simulated EMG recording for fixed or constant resistance. Superimposed over the electrical activity is a curve commonly referred to as a force, or tension, curve. Notice that the greatest amount of electrical activity occurs at the beginning of the lift and then tails off toward the end. This is due, in part, to the fact that it takes more energy to overcome inertia and get the weight moving. Once the weight is in motion, it is much easier to keep it moving; so less muscle tension is required. Recall that more electrical activity is synonymous with greater tension or contraction of the muscle. Consequently, most of the benefit with fixed resistances occurs in the beginning part of the lift.

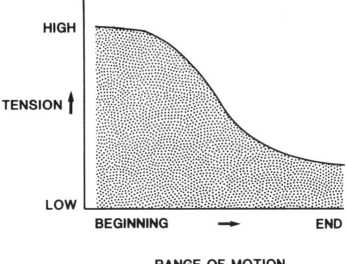

**Figure 5.2.** *Simulated force curve for fixed resistance. The curve is superimposed over the EMG recording. Notice that most of the tension is created in the beginning part of the lift.*

Free weights, dumbbells, some machines and calisthenics (own body weight) are examples of fixed resistances. With fixed resistances, once the resistance is selected, it does not change through the range of motion (ROM) of any lift. This is not the situation with variable and accommodating resistances.

As you look at the force curve, it is obvious that for a more effective contraction, the tail end of the curve needs to be raised upward. An ideal contraction would be one that produces constant tension in the muscle throughout the entire ROM and a subsequent straight line across the top of the force curve. Any drop of electrical activity from the straight line would signify a decrease in muscle tension.

## VARIABLE RESISTANCE

Variable resistance machines came into existence to try to address the shortcoming of fixed resistances. By manipulating the resistance to become harder through the ROM, it forces the muscle to contract harder during the latter stages of the ROM, and raises the tail end of the force curve upward. From Figure 5.3, you can see that the force curve created by variable resistance is an improvement over fixed resistance but still is not the straight line that would represent the ideal. By manipulating the resistance, variable resistance machines cause more tension in the muscle throughout the entire ROM. Theoretically, it is a better type of resistance to use over fixed or constant resistance. However, as will be discussed later in this chapter, the realities of applying this theoretical concept in the weight room may not produce the same effect.

Because the resistance is manipulated in variable resistance, to apply it usually re-

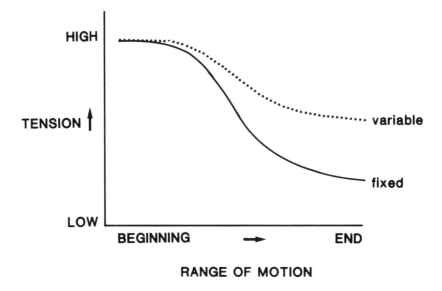

**Figure 5.3.** *Simulated force curve for variable resistance. Notice that the tail end of the curve is raised upward, thus signifying greater tension (than fixed resistance) being generated in the muscle through the last half of the ROM.*

quires some type of machine. It is impossible for free weights to represent a variable resistance station since the weights physically do not change through the ROM. A thick rubber band is a natural example of the variable resistance concept. As you stretch the band, the resistance becomes more difficult, which will result in greater tension being produced in the muscle at the end of the ROM. Remember that with variable resistance equipment, the resistance varies or changes through the ROM by only getting more difficult. The lifter has to adjust to this increase in resistance by increasing force or he will fail somewhere in the ROM.

## ACCOMMODATING RESISTANCE

In accommodating resistance, the resistance changes according to the amount of force that is exerted by the lifter. The resistance can become either easier or harder depending upon the strength of the lifter through the ROM. An accommodating resistance machine thus matches the amount of force that the muscle is able to exert with an equal amount of resistance. As Figure 5.4 illustrates, with accommodating resistance, there is constant tension in the muscle throughout the entire ROM, and a straight line across the top of the force curve. Theoretically, this is a more efficient muscle contraction than ones obtained with fixed or variable resistance equipment.

An easy way to distinguish the difference between variable and accommodating resistances is to remember that variable resistance only changes by getting harder (increasing the resistance) from the beginning of the lift to the end. Accommodating resistance, however, can become either harder or easier (more or less resistance) depending upon how

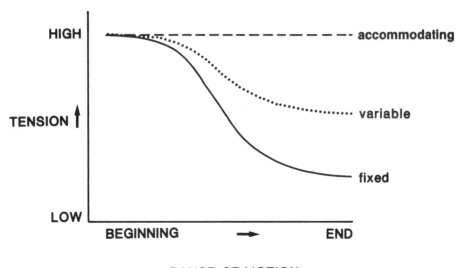

**Figure 5.4.** *Simulated force curve for accommodating resistance. Notice that the curve is now a straight line, which signifies constant tension being generated in the muscle throughout the entire ROM.*

much force the lifter exerts into the machine. So, with accommodating resistance, there is no failure. The individual always will be able to complete the lift regardless of the amount of force he can generate through the ROM. But, with variable and fixed resistances, the lifter has to adjust to the resistance that he selected. If he cannot exert enough force to overcome the resistance, then he will not be able to complete the lift.

Most of the tension generated by fixed resistance occurs at the _____ (BEGINNING, END) of a lift.

BEGINNING

Variable resistance tends to _____ (RAISE, LOWER) the tail end of the force curve _____ (UPWARD, DOWNWARD).

RAISE, UPWARD

With _____ (FIXED, VARIABLE, ACCOMMODATING) resistance, the weight or resistance does not change through the ROM of the lift.

FIXED

In _____ (VARIABLE, ACCOMMODATING) resistance, the resistance changes by only becoming more difficult through the ROM.

VARIABLE

In _____ (VARIABLE, ACCOMMODATING) resistance, the resistance can become easier or harder depending upon the amount of force exerted by the lifter.

ACCOMMODATING

What type of resistance results in a straight line across the top of a force curve?

ACCOMMODATING

What type of resistance results in constant tension being created in the muscle throughout the entire ROM?

ACCOMMODATING

Which type of resistance (FIXED, VARIABLE) will create more tension in the muscle?

VARIABLE

Which type of resistance is characterized by free weights?

FIXED

Which type of resistance would a thick rubber band represent?

VARIABLE

Whenever you select a resistance, which type of resistance are you *not* working with or *not* selecting?

ACCOMMODATING

---

## HOW VARIABLE RESISTANCE IS ACHIEVED

It is important to note how the various manufacturers of weight training equipment produce their variable resistance machines. If you can understand the concept behind a variable resistance machine, then you will be able to identify whether a piece of equipment is a variable or fixed resistance station simply by looking at it and moving the apparatus through its ROM. If it is a fixed resistance station, nothing will be done to alter the resistance through the ROM. However, if it is a variable resistance station, the resistance will have to be manipulated in some way that will result in it becoming greater as the lift is completed.

On most variable resistance machines, the weight or plate that you select does not change physically through the ROM (although the resistance the weight represents does change). The following are some examples of how manufacturers of weight training equipment manipulate their machines to make them variable resistance.

Universal machines use an interesting concept with their lever stations to make them variable resistance. In Figure 5.5, you can see that the difference between a fixed and a variable resistance station has to do with the weight stack and whether it slides out on the lever arm. If it slides out on the lever arm, it is variable resistance. If it does not, then it represents a fixed resistance station.

I like to illustrate this concept in my classes by using the following demonstration (Figure 5.6). First I take my hand and place it high up on a student's forearm and have him attempt to do a bicep curl or flex the elbow. Usually he can do this with little problem. I

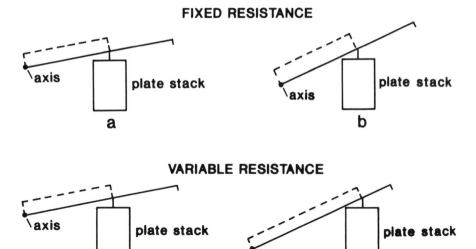

## FIXED RESISTANCE

axis — plate stack — **a**

axis — plate stack — **b**

## VARIABLE RESISTANCE

axis — plate stack — **a**

axis — plate stack — **b**

**Figure 5.5.** *Universal fixed and variable resistance stations. Notice that with variable resistance, the weights slide out on the lever arm, which increases the resistance.*

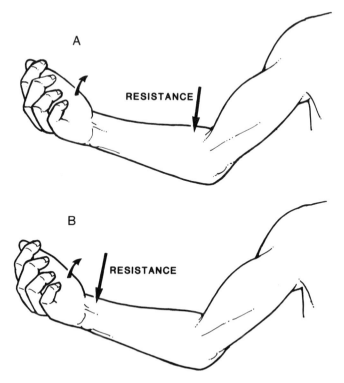

A

RESISTANCE

B

RESISTANCE

**Figure 5.6.** *Illustration showing that where the resistance is applied on the lever arm affects the ability to complete the movement. Although the same amount of resistance is applied in both examples, it is much harder to flex the elbow in (b) since the resistance is applied much further from the elbow joint (axis of rotation).*

*A picture of the Universal VR Squat Station. Notice the roller pin on top of the lever arm by the weight stack. As the lifter stands up, the weights will roll forward on the lever arm, creating the variable resistance. Courtesy of Universal Gym, Cedar Rapids, Iowa.*

then take my hand and place it farther down by the wrist, apply the same pressure, and have him attempt to do the same thing. It is only with great difficulty that he can complete the bicep curl. The increase in difficulty results from the simple fact that the resistance I applied was farther away from the axis, or elbow joint in this case. Although I did not apply any greater pressure, the resistance was greater because it was applied at a distance farther from the axis of rotation. The same outcome is achieved with the Universal lever system when the weight stack slides our farther on the lever arm. Although the weight does not physically change, the resistance it represents changes because of the location on the lever arm.

If the machines use some type of a pulley system, something will have to be done to that system to make it variable resistance (Figure 5.7). If the pulley system involves a spherical wheel (totally round) with no modifications, then it represents a fixed resistance station. However, if the wheel is odd shaped or elliptical, then it represents a variable resistance station. Nautilus uses this concept of the elliptical wheel with all of its weight training equipment. They refer to their wheel as a cam and they use chains instead of cable, but it is the same thing as a pulley system with an odd shaped or elliptical wheel.

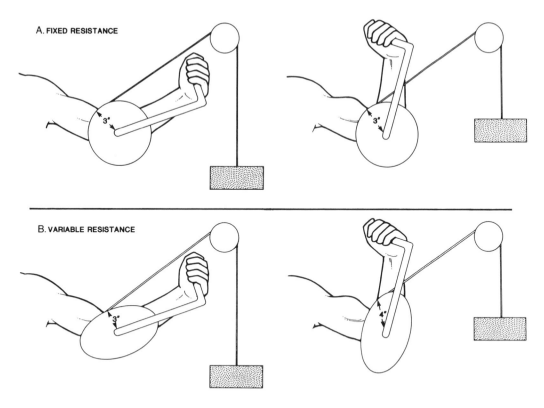

**Figure 5.7.** *Illustration showing with a pulley system how variable resistance is achieved. Notice that the wheel is elliptical (odd-shaped) rather than totally spherical. When the odd-shaped part of the wheel comes around, it is the same concept as applying the resistance further down the arm in a lever system.*

With a spherical wheel (Figure 5.7), all points along the wheel are equal distance from the center of rotation. However, with the elliptical wheel, it is obvious that some points on the wheel are not equal distance from the center of rotation. Thus, as the chain is rotated around the elliptical part of the wheel, the resistance will become greater (farther from the center of rotation). The wheel is positioned so that the elliptical portion will come into play during the latter portions of the ROM.

The Keiser Corporation manufactures another type of variable resistance machine based on air pressure. As the lever system is moved through its ROM, air is compressed in the cylinder, thus, increasing the resistance in the latter stages of the lift and making the station variable resistance.

## HOW ACCOMMODATING RESISTANCE IS ACHIEVED

Accommodating resistance machines use a slightly different system than variable resistance machines to match the force output generated by the lifter. Recall that with accommodating resistance, the resistance can become either harder or easier depending

*Spring-like devices and synthetic bands are natural methods of applying variable resistance. Here, the lifters are demonstrating three different uses of the Tiger Band. Tiger Bands are inexpensive, easily portable and effective in terms of developing strength and flexibility. Tiger Bands can make a significant contribution to weight rooms that have a limited amount of equipment. Courtesy of Tiger Bands, San Jose, CA.*

upon the force applied to the machine by the lifter. This is in contrast to variable or fixed resistance machines, where once a weight (resistance) is selected the lifter has to adjust to that weight throughout the entire ROM.

Lumex uses a cylinder filled with fluid and divided into two compartments to achieve their accommodating resistance. Between the compartments is an opening that can be controlled by the individual. The smaller the opening between the compartments, the slower the movement of the lever arm. The wider the opening, the faster the movement of the lever arm. As the lever arm is moved through its ROM, fluid is pushed from one compartment into the other. Accommodating resistance is accomplished by the back flow of pressure caused by the movement of fluid across the opening of the two compartments. The harder one pushes, the greater the back flow of fluid trying to get into the other compartment and the greater the resistance that will be encountered by the lifter. When the lifter cannot exert a lot of force, there is less backflow of fluid and, subsequently, less resistance encountered by the lifter. In this way, the machine is always able to match the force output generated by the lifter and achieve this accommodating resistance principle.

If the weight stack is attached to the lever arm in a stationary position (does not slide out), it is an indication of a _____ (FIXED, VARIABLE) resistance station.

FIXED

As the weight stack slides out further on the lever arm away from the axis of rotation, it will tend to _____ (INCREASE, DECREASE) the resistance that that weight represents.

INCREASE

A spherical wheel in a pulley system represents a _____ (FIXED, VARIABLE) resistance station.

FIXED

An elliptical wheel (odd-shaped) pulley system is an example of a _____ (FIXED, VARIABLE) resistance station.

VARIABLE

Accommodating resistance can either increase or decrease depending upon the _____ generated by the lifter.

FORCE

The _____ _____ of pressure of the fluid across the opening between the two compartments results in the ability of the resistance in accommodating to change in either direction.

BACK FLOW

# 6

# Weakest Point Principle

In Chapter 5, you learned about the various types of resistances (fixed, variable and accommodating) and the effectiveness of each one in creating tension throughout the entire range of motion (ROM). Accommodating resistance was clearly superior to the other two in that it created constant tension in the muscle through the ROM. The force curve was no longer a curve but rather a straight line, indicating the tension was not dropping off during the latter stages of the lift (Figure 6.1). In theory then, it would appear that everyone should be working out on accommodating resistance machines since they create more tension in the muscle. If accommodating machines aren't available (presently they are not being marketed for health spas and gyms), then variable resistance machines should be used because they are more efficient than fixed resistances (Figure 6.1). However, as you will learn from the ensuing discussion, the type of resistance matters less than the fact that you are creating tension in your muscles.

## VARYING STRENGTH CAPACITY—MUSCLE LENGTH/LEVERAGE

It is important to understand that in any exercise, you do not have the same strength capacity through the entire ROM. There are different areas in the ROM where your muscles can generate more or less force depending upon the following factors. First, as illustrated in Figure 6.2, a muscle exerts its greatest force when it is in a slightly stretched position. As it shortens or contracts, it loses its ability to generate as much force. This is due to the arrangement of the protein filaments in the muscle and their ability to maintain force as they slide past each other. Secondly, the mechanical alignment of the skeletal system and how the muscles are attached to it has to be considered. As you can see from Figure 6.3, the most mechanically efficient angle of pull for the bicep muscle during elbow flexion occurs when the elbow is flexed at 90 degrees. In any lift, there is going to be a point where, in terms of mechanical efficiency, the skeletal system lines up most advantageously and also a point where it lines up at an extreme disadvantage. All other points in the ROM bridge the gap between the two extremes in terms of mechanical efficiency. It is the result of both factors interacting together, muscle length and mechanical efficiency, that results in the fact that you are not able to generate an equal amount of force in your muscle through the entire ROM.

In Figure 6.4, you can see that for elbow flexion, the strongest point in the ROM occurs at approximately 110 degrees, which represents a compromise between the most mechanically efficient angle of pull (90 degrees) and muscle length (slightly stretched at 180 degrees). At 90 degrees, the muscle is contracted too much to generate maximum force at that position.

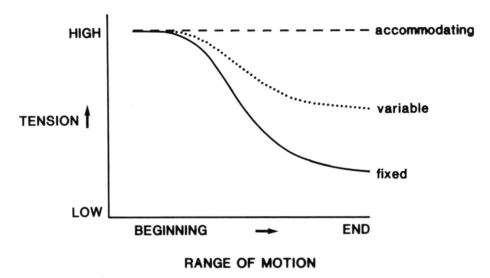

Figure 6.1. *Simulated force curves for fixed, variable and accommodating resistances.*

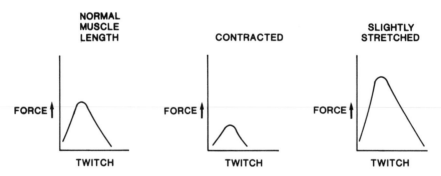

Figure 6.2. *Illustration showing three positions of muscle length. Notice when the muscle is slightly stretched, it generates the greatest amount of tension. As it shortens, it loses its ability to generate force.*

If there is a point in the ROM of any lift where you are the strongest (generating maximum force), there also must be a point where you are the weakest (generating only minimal force). In Figure 6.5, you can see that in a hypothetical example of elbow flexion, the weakest point occurs right at the beginning of the lift. Even though muscle-length is advantageous (slightly stretched), mechanical efficiency is so poor (180 degrees angle of pull) that it outweighs and out-factors muscle length. Consequently, the weakest point in the ROM of elbow flexion (bicep curl) occurs at the beginning of the lift. Although for many exercises the weakest point in the ROM occurs at the beginning, it may not hold true for all exercises.

## Weakest Point Limitation

Referring to Figure 6.5, it is obvious that the individual will only be able to lift 20 pounds regardless of how strong he is through other points in the ROM. Anything over

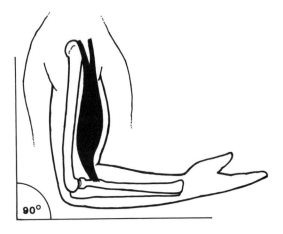

**Figure 6.3.** *Illustration showing, that for elbow flexion, the greatest angle of pull is 90 degrees.*

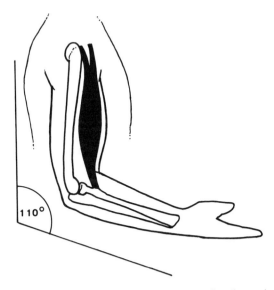

**Figure 6.4.** *When considering both muscle length and mechanical leverage system for elbow flexion, the greatest force is generated at approximately 110 degrees, which is a compromise of both factors.*

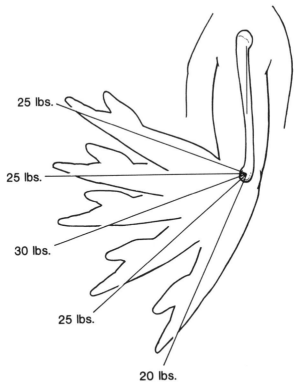

25 lbs.

25 lbs.

30 lbs.

25 lbs.

20 lbs.

**Figure 6.5.** *Hypothetical example of a vector diagram showing the weakest point in elbow flexion. In this example, the individual will only be able to successfully lift 20 pounds.*

20 pounds would result in failure in the beginning part of the lift. In Figure 6.6, you can see that even if the weakest point is moved to a different location in the ROM, it still is the limiting factor in determining how much weight the individual will lift. Although he may be stronger in the beginning part of the lift and handle more weight there, once he gets to the point in the ROM where he can only handle 20 pounds, he will fail if he is trying to work with anything more than that. Therefore, it is the *weakest* point in the ROM, with fixed or variable types of resistances, that will always determine the weight or resistance that is used by the lifter.

## Max Strength Test—Measurement of Weakest Point

What is actually determined in any strength test is *minimal* (weakest point) rather than maximal muscle strength. A chain is only as strong as its weakest link, and so are you through the ROM of any lift. Whenever you improve your strength, keep in mind that you have actually improved the ability of the weakest point in the ROM to handle that increase in weight. You are always limited by your weakest point and improvement is always determined by it.

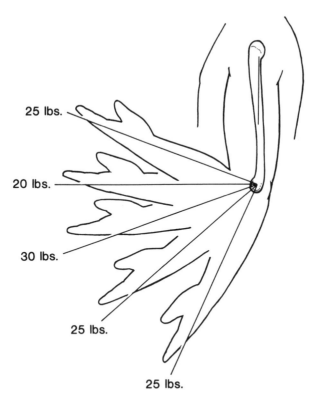

**25 lbs.**

**20 lbs.**

**30 lbs.**

**25 lbs.**

**25 lbs.**

**Figure 6.6.** *Hypothetical example of a vector diagram showing the weakest point being moved in the ROM for elbow flexion. Regardless of its position in the ROM, the weakest point is always the limiting factor in how much weight the individual will be able to lift.*

In any exercise, your muscles _____ (DO, DO NOT) have the same capacity for generating force (strength) through the entire ROM.

DO NOT

A muscle can exert its greatest force when it is slightly _____ (STRETCHED, SHORTENED).

STRETCHED

As a muscle shortens or contracts, it loses its ability to generate _____ .

FORCE

The mechanical alignment of the skeletal system _____ (DOES, DOES NOT) have an effect on the ability of the muscle to exert force through the ROM.

DOES

*The amount of weight that you are able to lift with free weights will always be governed by the weakest point in your ROM. Courtesy of Gold's Gym, Mountain View, CA.*

In any ROM, there will always be a point where you are the _____ and also a point where you are the _____ in terms of generating force.

STRONGEST, WEAKEST

If the weakest point in the ROM for a person doing a bicep curl is 10 pounds and the strongest is 30 pounds, what weight would he use to do the exercise (10, 20, 30 pounds)?

10 POUNDS

When you improve your strength in the bench press by 30 pounds over the course of a semester, what have you really improved?

WEAKEST POINT BY 30 POUNDS

## WHY THE TYPE OF RESISTANCE DOES NOT MATTER

Although the force curve illustrations clearly indicate that accommodating resistance is superior to fixed and variable in creating tension through the ROM, the reality is that accommodating resistance does not improve strength any more effectively than the other two types of resistances. The reason behind this apparent discrepancy has to do with the inability of any of the resistances to strengthen more effectively the weakest point.

## Fixed Resistance

Since the resistance in fixed remains the same throughout the entire ROM, the weakest point represents the only place in the ROM that is receiving a maximal stimulus or effort (Figure 6.7). All other points in the ROM, as you can see from the percents, are receiving less than a maximal stimulus. This does not mean that you are not developing strength in the other points of the ROM, but that you are strengthening them less than what they are capable of performing. It is only the weakest point in the ROM that is receiving the maximal stimulus.

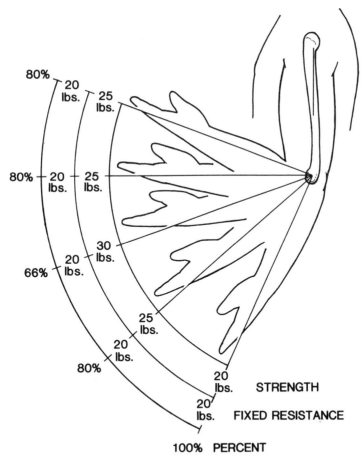

**Figure 6.7.** *Hypothetical example of a vector diagram for fixed resistance showing points in the ROM and what percent of their maximum potential is being utilized. Notice that the weakest point is the only point in the ROM that receives a maximal stimulus (100 percent).*

## Variable Resistance

In Figure 6.8, you can see that variable resistance improves the percentages through the ROM, however, it does not improve the weakest point any more so than fixed resistance (100 percent). You can make the point that, with variable resistance, you are strengthening other parts of the ROM more effectively than with fixed resistances. However, the case becomes academic since with either type of resistance you are still governed by the weakest point principle. Even though you are stronger in other parts of the ROM with variable resistance training, you are still limited by the 20 pounds (weakest point) with either type of resistance. If variable resistance could strengthen the weakest point in the ROM more effectively than fixed resistance, then it would be a definite advantage to work out with variable resistance equipment. However, whenever you work with fixed or variable resistances, the weakest point principle is always the limiting

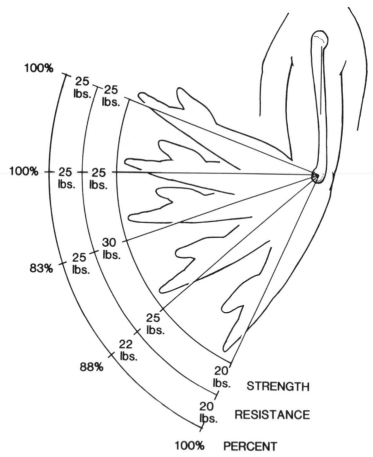

**Figure 6.8.** *Hypothetical example of a vector diagram for variable resistance showing points in the ROM and what percent of their maximum potential is being utilized. Notice that there is an improvement over fixed resistance.*

factor. Since neither resistance effectively improves the weakest point better than the other, there really is no advantage to working out with one over the other.

## Accommodating Resistance

When considering accommodating resistance (Figure 6.9), it is apparent that every point in the ROM is strengthened maximally or 100 percent. Since the machine matches force input with an equal amount of resistance, all points in the ROM receive a maximal stimulus. However, the weakest point is still not addressed any more effectively than with variable or fixed resistances; therefore, accommodating resistance is really not any more advantageous than fixed or variable resistances for improving strength.

Because the vast majority of resistances that you encounter in your every day routine are fixed and since none of the resistances effectively improves the weakest point any

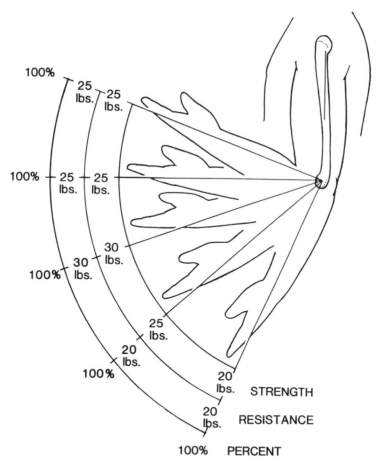

**Figure 6.9.** *Hypothetical example of a vector diagram for accommodating resistance showing points in the ROM and what percent of their maximum potential is being utilized. Notice that every point in the ROM is receiving a maximal stimulus (100 percent).*

better than the other, it really does not matter what type of resistance you use in your training program. Tension and overload are the keys to developing strength, not the type of resistance and equipment that you use.

## Testing for Strength—Consideration of Training Equipment

It is important to note that research has shown that testing for the improvement of strength should be done on the type of resistance that was used in the training program. For example, if the individual worked out with accommodating resistance equipment, then he should be tested on accommodating resistance machines to determine his improvement in strength. The same applies for variable and fixed resistance. Whenever you change the testing resistance from the training resistance, you confound the results of the improvement and may draw some false conclusions.

---

With fixed resistances, what point in the ROM is the only place to receive maximal (100 percent) stimulus?

WEAKEST POINT

With fixed resistances, other points in the ROM _____ (DO, DO NOT) receive any strength benefits.

DO

Variable resistance _____ (DOES, DOES NOT) strengthen the weakest point in the ROM anymore effectively than fixed resistance.

DOES NOT

With _____ (FIXED, VARIABLE) resistance, you can strengthen other points in the ROM more effectively.

VARIABLE

Accommodating resistance _____ (IS, IS NOT) any more effective in improving the weakest point than variable or fixed resistances.

IS NOT

The vast majority of resistances that you encounter during your everyday routine are primarily _____ (FIXED, VARIABLE, ACCOMMODATING).

FIXED

You should have confidence in knowing that the key to improving strength has more to do with creating _____ and _____ in the muscle than it has to do with what type of equipment you use.

TENSION/OVERLOAD

---

# 7

# Types of Muscle Contractions

There are three basic types of muscle contractions: (1) isometric, (2) isotonic, and (3) isokinetic. Depending upon the objectives of your weight training program, some or all of these contractions may be used appropriately. However, the most common contraction used is isotonic.

## ISOMETRIC CONTRACTION

An isometric contraction creates tension in the muscle without any movement. Muscles contract isometrically in the body to stabilize a particular body part while another body part is moving, or when a maximal resistance is met and the muscles cannot overcome the resistance so that no movement occurs at all. Often, when a lifter is completing the last repetition of a set, he may end up doing an isometric contraction because of muscle fatigue and need assistance from a spotter to complete the lift.

In the 1950s, isometric routines were very popular. A couple of German researchers (Hettinger and Muller) found that short daily isometric workouts could improve strength significantly. Closer scrutiny of their work, however, has shown some of the conclusions drawn from that study to be exaggerated. Isometric routines *can* develop strength, though. Remember, as long as sufficient tension is generated in a muscle, it will respond by getting stronger regardless of the type of contraction or resistance utilized.

### Routine

Although there are many variations of an isometric program, an acceptable routine would consist of holding a two-thirds to maximal contraction for six to 10 seconds and repeat it one to five times for each muscle group. Isometrics, in contrast to other training routines, can be done at least five times per week.

### Advantages

Since you can perform an isometric contraction against any immovable object, a routine can be done anywhere. Second, you don't need a lot of time to complete a total body isometric routine. Third, isometric contractions can serve a useful purpose in rehabilitating an injured muscle. Fourth, isometrics can be used to help overcome the "sticking point" in a lift. As you can see from Figure 7.1, the athlete can place the pins in a power rack in such a way that he ends up doing an isometric contraction at the precise point that he usually ends up failing in the range of motion (ROM) with conventional weights. This technique is mainly used by competitive lifters who are concerned with achieving their peak performance during a contest.

**Figure 7.1.** *An example of doing an isometric contraction at the lifter's sticking point, utilizing a power rack.*

## Disadvantages

One problem with isometrics is that the strength gained is specific to the joint angle in which the contraction was performed. For example, to gain strength throughout the entire ROM of the bicep muscle, you would have to do a number of isometric contractions at different joint angles (Figure 7.2). Since it would be impossible to work every joint angle, some points in the ROM would not be receiving an adequate stimulus.

A second disadvantage of isometrics is that there is no way to monitor the intensity of your effort. There is no feedback that can provide you with some objective measure, such as weights, to indicate when you have reached a two-thirds to maximal contraction. Consequently, you can never be certain that you are getting in the proper intensity with an isometric routine. Similarly, it is impossible to determine improvement with an isometric routine since you are contracting your muscles against immovable objects.

Third, it is difficult to obtain a total body workout with isometrics since immovable objects don't always make it easy to exercise certain muscle groups. For example, it takes a lot of creativity to adequately work the back and lower body isometrically.

Fourth, individuals that are hypertensive (having high blood pressure) definitely *should not* do isometrics since it tends to raise blood pressure to dangerous levels. Any type of muscle contraction will raise blood pressure; however, it appears that static contractions (isometrics) have a more deleterious effect on increasing blood pressure.

**Figure 7.2.** *Illustration showing how many different positions would have to be used isometrically to strengthen the entire bicep muscle.*

Figure 7.3 lists the specific advantages and disadvantages of an isometric routine. Since the disadvantages psychologically outweigh any of the physiological advantages, isometrics are primarily used today to rehabilitate an injured muscle.

---

## ISOMETRIC ROUTINE

| ADVANTAGES | DISADVANTAGES |
|---|---|
| • can be done anywhere | • strength gain specific to joint angle exercised |
| • time | • cannot monitor intensity of effort |
| • used in rehabilitation of injured muscle | • cannot determine improvement |
| • overcome "sticking" points | • difficult to obtain total body workout |
| • little expense involved for equipment | • increases blood pressure dramatically |

---

**Figure 7.3.** *The advantages and disadvantages of an isometric routine.*

An isometric contraction involves tension being created in the muscle _____ (WITH, WITHOUT) movement occurring.

WITHOUT

Isometric contractions _____ (CAN, CANNOT) develop strength.

CAN

While a muscle is immobilized from an injury, it _____ (MAY, MAY NOT) be helpful to do isometric contractions to help minimize the loss of strength.

MAY

An isometric contraction can help overcome the " _____ _____ " in a lift.

STICKING POINT

With an isometric contraction, strength gains are _____ (SPECIFIC, NON-SPECIFIC) to the joint angle exercised.

SPECIFIC

Isometric or static contractions can raise _____ _____ to exceedingly high levels.

BLOOD PRESSURE

A major problem with an isometric contraction is that you cannot monitor _____ or _____ of effort.

IMPROVEMENT, INTENSITY

## ISOTONIC CONTRACTION

An isotonic contraction creates tension in the muscle with movement. There are two phases to this contraction: the muscle shortening phase, called a *concentric* contraction, and the muscle lengthening phase, called an *eccentric* contraction.

When you perform an isotonic contraction, it is important to realize that you are working the same muscle group throughout the shortening (concentric) and lengthening (eccentric) phase of the movement. For example, when performing the bicep curl (Figure 7.4), you work the bicep muscle to flex the elbow (concentric or muscle shortening contraction). You also work the bicep muscle to bring the bar back to the starting position (eccentric or muscle lengthening contraction).

### Distinguishing Concentric and Eccentric Contractions

It may be helpful to think of an eccentric contraction, at least with free weights, as the phase that resists gravity. Whenever you are working against the effects of gravity, the muscle group that contracted concentrically to raise the weight is now lengthening and contracting eccentrically to lower the weight. With weight machines, the eccentric

**A. CONCENTRIC**
(Pulling)

**B. ECCENTRIC**
(Resting the pull)

**Figure 7.4.** *Isotonic contraction of the bicep muscle showing both phases, (a) concentric or muscle shortening, and (b) eccentric or muscle lengthening.*

phase of the contraction would occur as you return the bar or lever to its original position. Figure 7.5 provides you with some examples of concentric and eccentric contractions for four of the more popular exercises.

Another way to determine concentric from eccentric muscle contractions is to remember this simple rule that applies to both free weights and machines. *Pushing* or *pulling*

**Figure 7.5.** *Examples of isotonic concentric and eccentric contractions for the bench press, shoulder press, lat pulldown and leg press.*

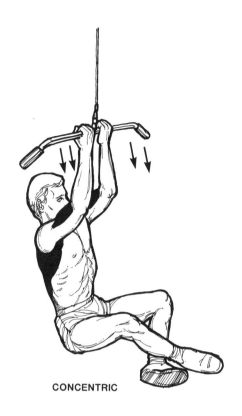

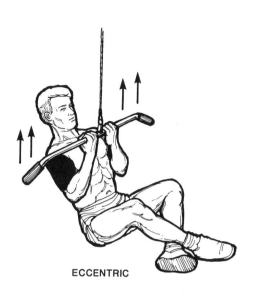

ECCENTRIC

CONCENTRIC

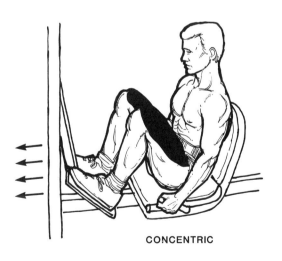

CONCENTRIC

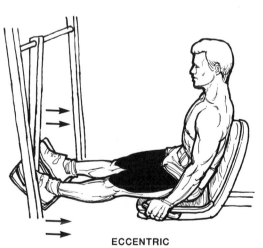

ECCENTRIC

will always represent the *concentric* phase of an isotonic muscle contraction while *resisting* the push or pull, will always represent the *eccentric* phase of the contraction.

## Benefit of Eccentric Contractions

It is important that you maintain tension in your muscles during the eccentric phase of the isotonic contraction since it has been proved that you can improve strength from that type of contraction just as well as the concentric or muscle shortening phase. In the late 1970s and early 1980s, it was popular to do "negatives" (eccentric contractions), particularly on the bench press, to increase muscle strength. The individual would put on more weight than he could lift concentrically (for example 50 pounds over his maximum), then slowly lower the bar to his chest. Spotters would help him lift the bar back to the starting position where he would again repeat the negative contraction two to three more times. This routine was effective in increasing muscle strength; however, it did result in extreme muscle soreness that impacted on the lifters' subsequent workouts. In addition, many lifters were injured from participating in negative training. Because of these two factors and the realization that it did not improve strength gains any more effectively than the traditional two phased isotonic contraction (concentric/eccentric), negative routines are rarely used by the competitive athlete today.

## Routine

A basic isotonic routine would consist of completing one to three sets of an exercise, performing six to 10 repetitions, two to three times per week. The reason for the range of repetitions is that most research studies have found effective strength gains utilizing anywhere from two to 10 repetitions. However, when performing a fewer number of repetitions, you lift heavier resistances, which could precipitate more muscle soreness and possible injury. For the average recreational lifter, a range of six to 10, or possibly even 12, repetitions per set is certainly reasonable and will produce the desired effect of increasing strength.

## Advantages

Figure 7.6 lists both the advantages and disadvantages of an isotonic routine. The two most distinguishing features of this type of routine is that you can monitor improvement and measure the intensity of a workout. For example, if your 1-RM on the bench press is 100 pounds and you did your sets at 80 pounds, you would be working out at 80 percent of your maximum. Since research studies have indicated that you need to lift at least 60 percent of your maximum to improve strength and encourage muscle hypertrophy, you would have instant feedback that your effort for that day was certainly within the bounds for obtaining these objectives. Also, if your 1-RM at the end of a certain time period is 150 pounds, it is easy to see how much you have improved. Psychologically, this ability to monitor improvement is extremely reinforcing and motivating for the lifter.

Another significant advantage of an isotonic routine is that it develops strength throughout the entire ROM of any movement. Although the strength gain is only maximal or 100 percent at the weakest point in the ROM (see Chapter 6), it still develops

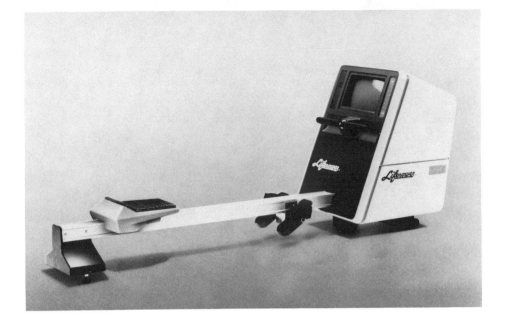

*Computers have enhanced the enjoyment of using selected pieces of fitness equipment. It will not be long before individual weight training stations will reflect this advancement in technology. Courtesy of Life Fitness Inc., Irvine, CA.*

## ISOTONIC ROUTINE

*ADVANTAGES*

- can determine intensity of effort

- can monitor and document improvement

- develops strength through the entire ROM

- more effective for muscle hypertrophy

- easier to work major muscle groups of the body

- psychologically more motivating than an isometric routine

*DISADVANTAGES*

- safety—more dangerous than an isometric routine

- expense

- more muscle soreness and greater chance of injury

- more time needed than an isometric routine

**Figure 7.6.** *The advantages and disadvantages of an isotonic routine.*

strength in other parts of the ROM, but at a submaximal level (less than 100 percent). Isotonic routines also tend to be much more effective in stimulating muscle hypertrophy than an isometric routine.

## Disadvantages

On the negative side, safety becomes a factor with an isotonic routine since it is possible to injure yourself by dropping weights or having the bar slip out of your hands. There is also much more muscle soreness associated with this type of routine (from the eccentric phase of the contraction), which could lead to a potential injury. In addition, an isotonic routine does require some out-of-pocket expense in terms of purchasing equipment for the home or joining a health club.

A type of contraction that generates tension with movement is _____ (ISOMETRIC, ISOTONIC, ISO-KINETIC).

ISOTONIC

The muscle shortening phase of an isotonic contraction is referred to as a _____ (CONCENTRIC, EC-CENTRIC) contraction.

CONCENTRIC

The muscle lengthening phase of an isotonic contraction is referred to as an _____ (CONCENTRIC, EC-CENTRIC) contraction.

ECCENTRIC

In what type of contraction (ISOMETRIC, ISOTONIC, ISOKINETIC) do you work the *same* muscle group through the entire ROM?

ISOTONIC

The term "negatives" is associated with which phase (CONCENTRIC, ECCENTRIC) of an isotonic contraction?

ECCENTRIC

The problem with "negatives" is that it causes a great deal of muscle _____ .

SORENESS

With isotonic contractions, you can monitor _____ and _____ of effort.

IMPROVEMENT, INTENSITY

An isotonic contraction develops strength _____ the entire ROM of any movement.

THROUGHOUT

Muscle soreness is associated more with which phase (CONCENTRIC, ECCENTRIC) of an isotonic contraction.

ECCENTRIC

## ISOKINETIC CONTRACTION

An isokinetic contraction is one in which the muscle generates tension and shortens but at a constant rate of speed. These are two distinguishing features that make an isokinetic contraction different from an isotonic contraction, although they both involve movement as a result of the muscle contracting.

First, an isokinetic contraction utilizes accommodating rather than fixed or variable resistance (see Chapter 5). Remember, in accommodating resistance, the force exerted by the lifter is matched with an equal amount of resistance by the machine. With fixed and variable resistances, the lifter has to adjust to the resistance he selected.

Second, an isokinetic contraction involves only the concentric, or muscle shortening, phase of an isotonic contraction. In order to complete a full ROM with an isokinetic machine, the lifter will have to push as well as pull. Remember, with an isotonic contraction, the lifter was either pushing or pulling during the concentric phase of the contraction, then resisting the push or pull during the eccentric phase of the contraction. The same muscle group was contracting in both phases of the lift.

With an isokinetic contraction, opposing muscle groups are brought into play in completing the ROM. For example, in doing a military press, the deltoid or shoulder muscle contracts concentrically to *push* the bar overhead. Now, however, instead of the deltoid muscle contracting eccentrically to lower the bar to the starting position (resisting the push), it is necessary for the lat muscle group (located on the mid-back) to contract concentrically to *pull* the bar back down to the starting position. Therefore, with an isokinetic contraction, you are working two opposing muscle groups (pushing and pulling) in one exercise.

An isokinetic routine is more efficient in that it reduces the amount of time that the lifter has to spend in the weight room. Instead of doing one exercise for the shoulders and then one for the back, both of these muscle groups are worked in the same isokinetic exercise.

## Routine

This routine is very similar to an isotonic routine in that you can do one to three sets of an exercise and six to 10 repetitions two to three times per week.

## Advantages

Figure 7.7 summarizes the major advantages and disadvantages of an isokinetic contraction. Although an isokinetic contraction does develop strength more effectively through the entire ROM, the fact that it does not improve strength in the weakest point any more effectively than an isotonic contraction makes that advantage somewhat academic (see Chapter 6).

---

### ISOKINETIC ROUTINE

*ADVANTAGES*

- develops maximal strength throughout entire ROM

- works opposing muscle groups in same exercise—more efficient timewise

- used for rehabilitation of an injured muscle

- effective at faster movement speeds for developing strength

- less muscle soreness because it eliminates eccentric phase of contraction

*DISADVANTAGES*

- extremely expensive

- not mass marketed in health clubs yet

---

**Figure 7.7.** *The advantages and disadvantages of an isokinetic routine.*

Isokinetic contractions are very beneficial for rehabilitating an injury (see Chapter 14). And, since they do not involve the eccentric or lengthening phase of a muscle contraction, the potential for developing muscle soreness is much less. In addition, isokinetic contractions appear to be more effective in terms of creating tension in the muscle at faster speeds than isotonic contractions. With weights (isotonic contraction), if you want to do an explosive movement, you have to select a resistance that is very light in order to obtain the speed you desire. EMG recordings of these types of contractions have indicated that most or all of the tension produced occurs in the beginning part of the lift with a marked drop after that point. It appears that once the weight is put in motion, momentum forces take over and very little work or tension is created in the muscle. With an isokinetic contraction, however, the faster the lifter tries to move the lever system, the harder he pushes, which results in greater resistance. The end result is that greater tension is produced in the muscle at faster speeds of movement with isokinetic contractions.

## Disadvantages

Isokinetic machines are extremely expensive and cost prohibitive for most health clubs to purchase. Also, the machines have not been designed to be marketed to the general populace. Consequently, most of the market for isokinetic equipment has been in rehabilitation and sports medicine. In the near future, however, you will probably see more of this type of equipment being used by the health clubs.

---

Which type of muscle contraction (ISOTONIC, ISOKINETIC) involves a fixed rate of speed?

ISOKINETIC

Which type of muscle contraction (ISOMETRIC, ISOTONIC, ISOKINETIC) utilizes accommodating resistance?

ISOKINETIC

Which type of muscle contraction (ISOMETRIC, ISOTONIC, ISOKINETIC) utilizes fixed and variable resistances?

ISOTONIC

With an isokinetic contraction, you _____ (DO, DO NOT) have an eccentric or muscle lengthening phase of the contraction.

DO NOT

Which type of muscle contraction (ISOMETRIC, ISOTONIC, ISOKINETIC) works the opposing muscle groups during the same exercise?

ISOKINETIC

What type of muscle contraction (ISOMETRIC, ISOTONIC, ISOKINETIC) requires you to push and pull to complete the ROM?

ISOKINETIC

If you push or pull, then have to resist the push or pull to get the weights back to the starting position, what type of muscle contraction (ISOMETRIC, ISOTONIC, ISOKINETIC) have you just performed?

ISOTONIC

Resisting the push or pull is what phase of an isotonic contraction (CONCENTRIC, ECCENTRIC)?

ECCENTRIC

Which type of muscle contraction (ISOMETRIC, ISOTONIC, ISOKINETIC) is beneficial in terms of rehabilitating an injured muscle?

ISOMETRIC/ISOKINETIC

Which type of muscle contraction (ISOMETRIC, ISOTONIC, ISOKINETIC) is more effective at creating tension at faster speeds of movement?

ISOKINETIC

---

# 8

# Understanding the Neuromuscular System

Muscle will not contract and generate tension unless it receives an electrical impulse from the nervous system. Consequently, it is important to have some knowledge of the neuromuscular (nervous and muscle) system to understand how it affects strength development.

We know that muscle needs to be innervated or stimulated by the nervous system in order to contract because individuals who have severed or traumatized their spinal columns are often left paralyzed. Nervous impulses are still being sent down the spinal column by the brain; however, they cannot get past the lesion or damaged area and, as a result, muscles below that point are not able to contract. Depending upon where the injury occurs to the spinal column (high or low), the result could be either a paraplegic (loss of use of legs), a quadriplegic (loss of use of both arms and legs) or even death due to paralysis of the muscles that are involved in respiration (breathing).

Strokes are another condition that draw attention to the importance of the neuromuscular system. Because of a lack of oxygen to the brain, nervous tissue is damaged with the result that normal movement patterns are impaired. Again, there is an interruption of the neuromuscular system (this time with the brain, not the spinal column) with the consequences leading to partial or total paralysis.

Muscle has no preference regarding how it receives an electrical impulse to start the contraction process. The impulse can be transmitted internally by the nervous system or externally by mild electrical current. The key factor is that as long as it receives an electrical impulse, it will respond by contracting and generating tension.

Researchers are using this principle (external electrical stimulation) to help the paralyzed become more mobile. In some pioneering work at Wright State University in Ohio, individuals have been able to ride three-wheeled bicycles and walk with assistance. With the aid of a computer, mild electrical currents are run through the leg muscles to simulate the contraction patterns involved in walking and bicycling. Although the original movements were somewhat awkward and jerky, subsequent refinements have significantly improved upon these patterns.

---

Muscle will not contract or shorten unless it receives an _____ impulse.

ELECTRICAL

In humans, this electrical impulse comes from the _____ system.

NERVOUS

People who have traumatized their spinal columns are often left _____ .

PARALYZED

What other condition can result in interruption of the impulses coming from the brain to the muscles?

STROKE

The problem with traumatic injury to the spinal column is that the brain is still sending down impulses for the muscles to contract; however, these impulses cannot get past the lesion in the spinal column to _____ the muscles below that point.

STIMULATE OR ACTIVATE

Muscle also will contract if it receives an electrical impulse from an _____ source.

EXTERNAL OR OUTSIDE

Whenever a muscle receives an electrical impulse, regardless of the source, it will respond by _____ .

CONTRACTING OR SHORTENING

Researchers are currently experimenting with _____ that send electrical impulses to the leg muscles of paralyzed individuals to assist them in walking and riding three-wheeled bicycles.

COMPUTERS

---

## Relationship to Weight Training

In resistive type exercise (weight training), you are sending impulses from your nervous system to your muscles to contract. The greater the resistance that is to be overcome, the greater the number of impulses traveling from the brain to the muscle. The end result of this action will be a more forceful contraction since more of the fibers in the muscle will be contracting simultaneously. Weight training is actually *training* your neuromuscular system to become more efficient at sending down impulses from the brain. The initial gains in strength during the first three to six weeks on a weight training program are primarily attributable to this increase in neuromuscular efficiency since the synthesis of new muscle tissue has yet to occur.

To a certain extent, we have some control over the number of impulses being sent from the brain to the muscle. If we perceive an object to be heavy that we are attempting to lift, we send down more impulses from the brain to increase the amount of force that our muscles exert. Sometimes we make errors in judgement. When the resistance is less than we had anticipated, since we had already prepared our muscles to exert more force, we overreact.

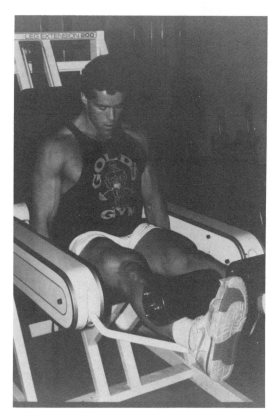

*In weight training, you are conditioning the neuromuscular system to become more efficient at sending impulses from the brain to the contracting muscle to generate greater force. Courtesy of Gold's Gym, Mountain View, CA.*

## Coordination

Some people have much greater control over their neuromuscular systems than others. When we talk about a coordinated athlete, what we really are talking about is his ability to control or coordinate his neuromuscular system. For example, if a group of 30 recreational athletes saw a perfect demonstration of how to hit a tennis ball, there would probably be 30 different interpretations of that swing. Those individuals that came the closest to duplicating that stroke would have demonstrated a greater ability of neuromuscular control.

## Natural Athletes

A key that this ability to control the neuromuscular system is genetic is in the label applied to people gifted in this area as natural athletes. The term "natural" implies that these athletes were born with this control and that, regardless of the sport or activity,

*The skill and agility needed to become a successful Olympic lifter requires a tremendous degree of coordination between the nervous and muscular systems.*

they would excel at it. Although practice will make individuals with less coordination more proficient, it will never get them to the level of those born with this ability. If practice could make up the difference, then anyone could be a professional in any sport, as long as he put in the training. Since we know that this does not occur, other factors such as genetic ability have to be considered.

Fortunately, in weight training, being coordinated is not as critical a factor as it is in other types of skill activities or sports. The key is to put a stress on the muscle and have it adapt by getting stronger. With training, the neuromuscular system may become slightly more coordinated; however, it will definitely become more efficient at sending impulses from the brain to the contracting muscle, which will result in greater strength.

---

The more electrical impulses coming from the brain, the _____ (GREATER, LESSER) the force that will be exerted by the contracting muscle.

GREATER

In weight training, you are actually training your neuromuscular system to become more _____ at sending impulses to the contracting muscle.

EFFICIENT

The initial gains in strength at the beginning of a weight training program are primarily attributable to an _____ in neuromuscular efficiency, not an increase in muscle size.

INCREASE

We _____ (CAN, CANNOT) consciously control impulses sent by the nervous system out to the contracting muscle.

CAN

This control becomes readily apparent when you go to lift up something that you _____ to be very heavy and wind up embarrassed because it was much lighter than you thought.

PERCEIVED

People who have good control or coordination of their neuromuscular system are often times referred to as _____ _____ .

NATURAL ATHLETES

This ability to control your neuromuscular system is more a function of _____ (GENETICS, PRACTICE).

GENETICS

Although practice will improve control over the neuromuscular system, it can never make up the difference between someone who is truly _____ in this area and someone who is not.

GIFTED

---

## THE MOTOR UNIT

The basic unit tying the nervous and muscle system together is called the "motor unit." This is the unit that transfers impulses from the brain and spinal column to the individual fibers in the muscle that initiate the contraction process. A motor unit consists of a *motor nerve* and all the *muscle fibers* that it innervates (stimulates) or attaches to (Figure 8.1).

It is important that you are able to distinguish between the terms "motor nerve" and "motor unit." A *motor nerve* is simply a nerve that carries *impulses* from the spinal column to the *muscle*. A *motor unit* is more encompassing in that it not only consists of a motor nerve but *also* all the *muscle fibers* that it attaches to.

There are many motor units involved in activating a muscle. For illustrative purposes, Figure 8.2 shows only a few of them. However, in the large muscles of the leg, there can be several dozen motor units that activate the entire muscle.

A motor nerve may attach to a few or to many muscle fibers depending upon its function. In large muscles involving rather simple movements (such as the thigh), one

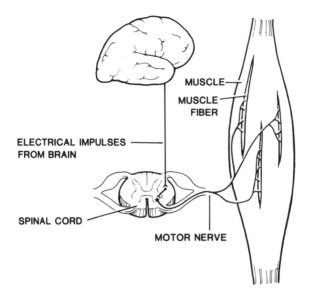

**Figure 8.1.** *Diagram of the motor unit showing the motor nerve and muscle fibers that it innervates (attaches to).*

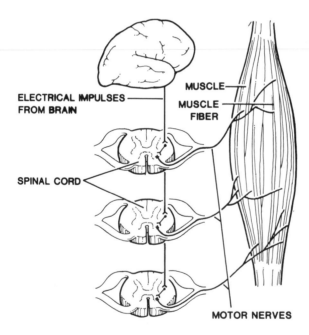

**Figure 8.2.** *Diagram showing several motor units activating a muscle. In essence, there can be several dozen or more motor units activating one muscle.*

motor nerve may activate anywhere up to 1,000 muscle fibers. In more complex movements such as those found in the eye, one motor nerve may activate as few as five to 10 muscle fibers. With more complex movements, fewer muscle fibers are attached to each motor nerve to provide the diversity of movement.

## THE ALL OR NONE PRINCIPLE

The all or none principle governs the action of the motor unit. Whenever an impulse travels down a motor nerve, *all muscle fibers attached* to that *nerve* will *contract* or shorten *maximally*. There is no partial contraction of muscle fibers. There is either a 100 percent shortening or nothing at all (all or none).

### The Ability to Vary Force

The ability to contract our muscles with different degrees of force depends upon the number of motor units that are activated (as well as the frequency with which motor units are activated). With light resistances, only a few motor units will be activated, which means that only a few muscle fibers are doing the work. With heavier resistances, more motor units are brought into play, resulting in more muscle fibers shortening at the same time. Since it is the shortening of muscle fibers that creates force, the muscle will be able to exert greater force when more fibers contract at the same time. Thus, it is important to remember that we vary the force of our muscle contractions by activating more or fewer motor units, not by causing partial or weak contraction of individual muscle fibers.

If you can recall from Chapter 5 (Types of Resistances), an electromyogram (EMG) measures electrical activity produced by the muscle. The electrical activity that the EMG records is actually the firing of the motor units when the muscle is contracting or shortening. Where the resistance dropped off in the ROM of a lift due to momentum and inertia, the EMG recording also dropped off since fewer motor units were being recruited. Where the resistance was greater, more motor units were being called into play, and, therefore, more electrical activity showed on the EMG recording.

If the situation existed wherein one motor nerve activated all of the fibers in a muscle (Figure 8.3), there would be no reason for you to train with weights. Every time that nerve was activated, the end result would be a maximal contraction, since all of the fibers within the muscle would be shortening simultaneously. Because you couldn't activate any more muscle fibers with training, there would be no reason to work out.

This situation would be ideal for activities that required maximum strength. However, daily living experiences would become very difficult. Since you would get a maximal contraction every time you activated a motor unit, you would lose the ability to vary the force of your muscle contractions. Can you imagine what brushing your teeth, eating or putting in contact lenses would be like? Fortunately, we do have many motor units innervating a muscle that gives us the ability to activate more or fewer of them depending upon the task we are trying to accomplish. Athletes involved in strength sports are training their neuromuscular systems through resistive exercise to fire as many motor units as possible upon demand. The more successful they become at this function, the greater the improvement in strength that will be realized.

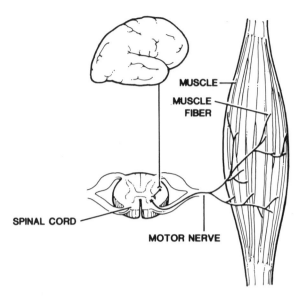

**Figure 8.3.** *Hypothetical example showing one motor nerve innervating the entire muscle. In this situation, a maximal contraction would result every time the motor unit was activated.*

---

The basic unit that integrates the nervous and muscular system is called the ____ ____.

MOTOR UNIT

A motor *unit* consists of a motor ____ and all the ____ ____ that are attached to it (that it activates).

NERVE, MUSCLE FIBERS

Motor *nerves* carry impulses ____ (TOWARD, AWAY FROM) the brain.

AWAY FROM

The more motor *units* activated in a muscle, the ____ (GREATER, LESSER) the amount of force generated by the contracting muscle.

GREATER

In large muscles of the body that perform rather simple movements, one motor *nerve* may activate as many as ____ muscle fibers.

1,000

With muscles that are involved in complex movements such as the eye, one motor *nerve* may activate as few as ____ to ____ muscle fibers.

FIVE, 10

There are _____ (MANY, FEW) motor *units* that activate a large muscle such as the thigh.

MANY

Our ability to generate different degrees of force in a muscle is dependent upon our ability to activate many or _____ motor units.

FEW

The greater the resistance that is to be overcome by a muscle, the _____ (GREATER, FEWER) the number of motor units that will be activated.

GREATER

The _____ or _____ principle refers to the following phenomenon: whenever an impulse travels down a motor nerve, all of the muscle fibers associated with that nerve will shorten or contract maximally or 100 percent.

ALL, NONE

If a muscle had only one motor unit activating it, the end result would be a _____ contraction each time that motor unit was fired.

MAXIMAL

Weightlifters are trying to activate _____ (MANY, FEW) motor units at one time in order to generate as much force (strength) as possible from their muscles.

MANY

---

# IMPORTANCE OF TRAINING SPECIFICITY

Recall from Chapter 2 that it is important to lift in a specific manner to gain strength (specificity principle). In performing many repetitions to fatigue using a light weight (muscle endurance), most of the motor units within the muscle are brought into play but not at the same time. As the repetitions continue, some of the motor units become fatigued while others are activated to take over the workload. Since you are never training the neuromuscular system to activate motor units at the same time, it will be very difficult for you to realize significant increases in strength with this type of routine.

When an impulse travels down a motor nerve repeatedly (such as in lifting weights), it becomes easier for that nerve pathway to be activated in the future. Consequently, one of the adaptations that occurs with weight training is the neuromuscular systems increasing efficiency at firing motor nerves. Lifting heavy resistances forces the muscle to recruit additional motor units and activate them simultaneously.

## Bad Habits

The fact that nerve pathways are easier to activate after repeated stimulation is a major reason behind the difficulty encountered in attempting to break a bad habit. It appears that once the neuromuscular pathway is established in learning a new skill, it is extremely difficult to develop new motor unit recruitment patterns. Consequently, if bad

*Since machines do not develop muscles that assist the primary mover in performing a lift, most competitive athletes use free weights as the basis of their training programs. These athletes also use machines for certain movements, but the majority of their program is done with free weights. Courtesy of Universal Gym, Cedar Rapids, Iowa.*

habits were developed early in an athlete's career, it is hard for that person to ever develop proper technique. In weight training, fortunately, learning the proper lifting techniques doesn't require a lot of complex movements.

## Women's Neuromuscular Efficiency

Research studies have indicated that women may be more effective than men at increasing the efficiency of motor unit recruitment with training. Since their improvement in strength cannot be attributed to a significant increase in muscle size, the only plausible explanation is that they are able to activate more motor units and have more of their muscle fibers contract simultaneously. Fortunately, that is exactly what most women desire from a weight training program: an increase in muscle strength, tone and definition without an increase in muscle size (hypertrophy).

---

In developing muscle _____ (STRENGTH, ENDURANCE), you are training your neuromuscular system to activate some motor units as others get fatigued and stop working.

ENDURANCE

Once a motor nerve is repeatedly activated, that motor nerve will become _____ (EASIER, HARDER) to activate in the future.

EASIER

Once a neuromuscular pathway is established, it becomes _____ (EASIER, HARDER) to activate this pathway in the future.

EASIER

Bad habits are the result of establishing _____ (CORRECT, INCORRECT) neuromuscular pathways in the process of learning a new movement pattern.

INCORRECT

It appears that women may have a better ability than men to _____ motor units since their improvement in strength over a period of time is not the result of a significant increase in muscle size.

ACTIVATE OR RECRUIT

# 9

# Nervous System Influences
# Over Muscle

## EXCITATORY AND INHIBITORY IMPULSES

There are two basic nervous system influences over muscle: *excitatory* impulses, which result in muscle contraction; and *inhibitory* impulses, which result in muscle relaxation. In the normal resting state, inhibitory influences predominate since muscle is relaxed, not contracted. It is only when movement is desired that excitatory impulses coming from the brain overpower the inhibitory influences, resulting in a muscle contraction.

### Voluntary Control of Muscle

Muscle is often referred to as voluntary muscle since it is under our control. When we want to move, we send excitatory impulses to the muscles, which result in a contraction and movement of the skeletal system. When we don't want to move, the inhibitory influences keep the muscles in a relaxed state. Unfortunately, with damage to the brain, individuals often lose this ability to control their muscles. Excitatory impulses may either be sent to the muscles at any time, resulting in spastic movements, or continually transmitted, which results in a constant state of contraction. With either condition, voluntary control of muscle is lost, which ends up making the easiest of chores extremely difficult, if not impossible, to do.

---

The two basic influences over muscle are _____ and _____.

EXCITATORY, INHIBITORY

In the normal resting condition of muscle, _____ influences predominate since the muscle is in a relaxed state.

INHIBITORY

When we want to move or contract our muscles, _____ impulses override the inhibitory control over our muscles, which result in a contraction.

EXCITATORY

Muscle is sometimes referred to as _____ muscle, which means we can control it and have it contract upon our will or command.

VOLUNTARY

---

# LIFE-THREATENING CONDITIONS

It is interesting that the potential for developing strength is never fully achieved in the human species. In times of extreme duress, average individuals have been known to demonstrate extraordinary feats of strength, making it apparent that the potential for such strength was always within their means. It is also obvious that nothing less than an extremely traumatic event preceded such actions.

It appears that in a state of shock or high arousal several things occur simultaneously in the body that allow muscles to exert this tremendous degree of force. First, the hormone *adrenaline* is released into the blood stream to enhance muscle contraction. Second, the brain sends a tremendous volley of excitatory impulses to the muscles, which causes them to contract harder. Third, receptors that prevent muscle from contracting too hard and injuring itself are overridden. As a result of all these actions, the muscles of the body are able to demonstrate their true strength potential.

# NERVOUS SYSTEM AROUSAL

It is apparent that when the nervous system is agitated or in a high state of arousal, muscle responds by being able to exert a tremendous amount of force. It really doesn't matter what causes the arousal in the nervous system in terms of eliciting this strength potential. For example, people on excitatory drugs such as PCP, having seizures or in extreme anger or danger can all demonstrate extraordinary degrees of strength regardless of how weak or frail they may be. In all of these conditions, the nervous system is in a highly aroused or excited state due to circumstances that the individual is confronting.

## Psyching Up

Athletes are well aware that "psyching up" before a contest results in a better performance, particularly in sports requiring great efforts of strength or power. Psyching up is simply a self-induced method of exciting the nervous system. Many weight trainers like to exercise with loud music blaring in the background because they are able to lift more weight and get in a better work out. Whether they realize it, the music simply represents an artificial method of exciting the nervous system, which results in their exhibiting more strength. Even in this "psyched up" state, however, the body doesn't exhibit all of its true strength potential since athletic achievements fall far short of the achievements that occur with non-athletic individuals in times of extreme duress.

# PURPOSE OF INHIBITORY CONTROL

Muscle has the potential to generate so much force that it could actually fracture bone and "pull" tendons and muscle tissue. To counteract this potential and protect the body from harm, there are inhibitory receptors (called Golgi Tendon Organs) located in the tendons of muscles. Whenever muscle creates too much tension, these receptors are activated and inhibit the muscle from contracting any harder. Weight training has a tendency to desensitize these receptors so they are not so quickly activated. Because tendons

**Figure 9.1.** Psyching up plays an important part in any activity where max strength is desired. Here an Olympic lifter demonstrates intense concentration and focus before attempting his lift. Courtesy of the United States Weightlifting Federation. (Bruce Klemens photo)

grow stronger with training, it will take a more forceful contraction to activate the receptors. As a consequence, muscle is able to exert more force with training partly due to the desensitizing effect on the inhibitory receptors in the tendons.

During a state of extreme duress, _____ (name of a hormone) is released into the bloodstream, resulting in a more forceful muscle contraction.

ADRENALINE

Also, in this state of duress, _____ control of the muscles is overpowered by excitatory impulses sent from the brain.

INHIBITORY

It seems that if the nervous system is in a high state of _____, muscles are able to generate more force.

AROUSAL OR AGITATION

Consequently, athletes who " _____ " themselves up are really enhancing their ability to generate force from their muscles.

PSYCH

Even the greatest athletic achievements fall far _____ of the achievements of non-athletic individuals in times of extreme duress.

SHORT

The reason there are inhibitory influences over muscle is to prevent _____ or harm to the body.

INJURY

Muscle tissue has the potential to generate so much force that it could actually _____ bone.

FRACTURE

The inhibitory influences of muscle that prevent it from contracting too hard are found in the _____ of the muscle.

TENDONS

Whenever a muscle generates so much force that it could potentially do harm to the body, the inhibitory receptors are _____, which prevents the muscle from contracting any harder.

ACTIVATED

Since weight training not only strengthens muscle but also the tendons associated with that muscle, it will become _____ (HARDER, EASIER) for the inhibitory receptors to be activated in the future.

HARDER

Weight training tends to have a _____ effect on inhibitory receptors resulting in greater force being exerted by muscle.

DESENSITIZING

# 10

# The Structure of Muscle

Now that you have some degree of understanding of the neuromuscular system, it is time to take a closer look at muscle to see how it is structured. Gaining such insight will provide you with a better idea of how muscles function and respond to different types of training programs.

Basically, muscles move the skeletal system because they are attached to it in such a way that, when contracted or shortened, they pull one body part closer to or farther away from another body part. This action occurs because muscles cross over joints. As you can see from Figure 10.1, when the bicep muscle does not cross over the elbow joint, there is no way for it to have any effect on that joint. However, as you can see in Figure 10.2, when the bicep muscle shortens this time, it will result in elbow flexion since it does cross over the elbow joint. This same principle applies for most joints in the body. Muscles in the forearm move the wrist because their tendons cross over the wrist joint (Figure 10.3). Muscles in the thigh move the knee, and muscles in the calf move the ankle, because their tendons cross over the knee and ankle joints, respectively (Figure 10.3).

The structure of muscle is very organized. If you look at Figure 10.4, you can see that muscle is actually compartmentalized into bundles of fibers, the smaller ones incorporated into the larger ones. All of these bundles, whether large or small, are interconnected or tied to the bundles surrounding them by a thin sheath of fascia, or connective tissue. Consequently, every bundle in the muscle, no matter how large or small, is inherently tied into the entire structure of the muscle, which ensures that it will act as one unit. Although only a few fibers may be contracting in overcoming a light resistance, the entire muscle shortens because of this fascial sheath connection.

Tendons are actually all of the fascia within a muscle coming together at either end to connect the muscle to the skeletal system (Figure 10.5). They are responsible for transferring force generated by the muscle to the skeletal system. interestingly, weight training not only strengthens muscle but also the tendons of the muscles exercised. If tendons did not get stronger with training, muscle would be limited by how much force the tendons could withstand.

Muscles have to _____ over a joint in order to have any effect on it.

CROSS

Muscles in the forearm move the _____ (WRIST, ELBOW).

WRIST

The bicep muscle is responsible for _____ (WRIST, ELBOW) flexion.

ELBOW

The bundles and fibers in a muscle are connected to each other by a thin sheath of _____.

FASCIA OR CONNECTIVE TISSUE

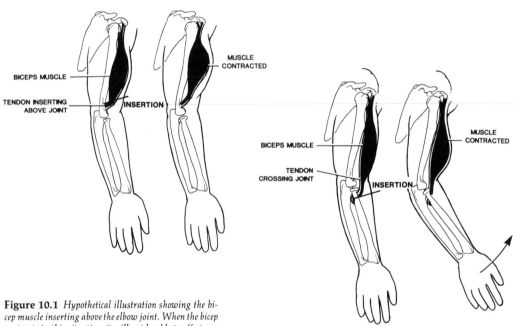

**Figure 10.1** *Hypothetical illustration showing the bicep muscle inserting above the elbow joint. When the bicep contracts in this situation, it will not be able to affect any movement on the elbow joint.*

**Figure 10.2.** *Illustration showing the bicep muscle inserting below the elbow joint. In this situation, the elbow will be flexed when the bicep contracts.*

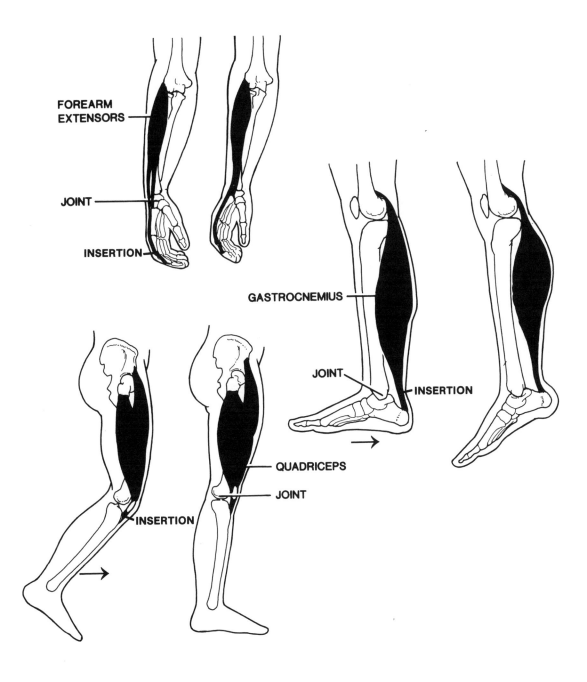

**Figure 10.3.** *Illustrations of the forearm, thigh and calf muscles showing what joints they cross over and, thus, move.*

The _____ of a muscle actually represents all of the fascia within a muscle coming together at either end.

TENDON

Strengthening muscle through a weight training program also _____ the tendons associated with that muscle.

STRENGTHENS

---

## MUSCLE STRUCTURE

As mentioned earlier, muscle is composed of many bundles of fibers (Figure 10.4). The larger bundles are referred to as fasciculi. Contained within the fasciculi are many smaller bundles that are referred to as muscle fibers or muscle cells. The largest of these fibers have the thickness of a human hair, so it is important to realize that they are microscopic in nature. Contained within the muscle fiber are smaller bundles called myofibrils ("myo" means muscle). Found within the myofibril are hundreds of tiny threadlike protein filaments. So, it is important to keep in mind that even the largest muscles are still composed of tiny, microscopic structural protein filaments.

Figure 10.4 also shows a simulation of a highly magnified section of a protein filament teased out from a myofibril. As you can see, it contains two specific proteins, actin and myosin, arranged in a row of box-like structures. The thicker and darker protein in the middle of the boxes is myosin, while the thinner, threadlike protein on the sides of the boxes is actin. In essence, then, muscle is really composed of these two proteins arranged in a very specific pattern.

## MUSCLE CONTRACTION

To understand how a muscle contracts, it is necessary to take a look at a sarcomere, which represents one box in the row of box-like structures (Figure 10.6). The protein filaments contained within the myofibril are literally composed of rows upon rows of sarcomeres. A sarcomere then represents the smallest contractile element within a muscle. As you can see from Figure 10.6, when a muscle receives an impulse from the nervous system, the thicker myosin proteins in the middle of the sarcomere pull the actin filaments toward the center of the unit. This reduces the border of the sarcomere as noted in Figure 10.6. Of course, this is occurring in every sarcomere throughout the protein filament with the end result being the entire protein strand reduced in size significantly (Figure 10.7). Figure 10.8 gives you some idea of how the sarcomeres shorten within a muscle. This description of how a muscle contracts is called the "sliding filament theory" and is the most widely accepted one to date in the scientific community.

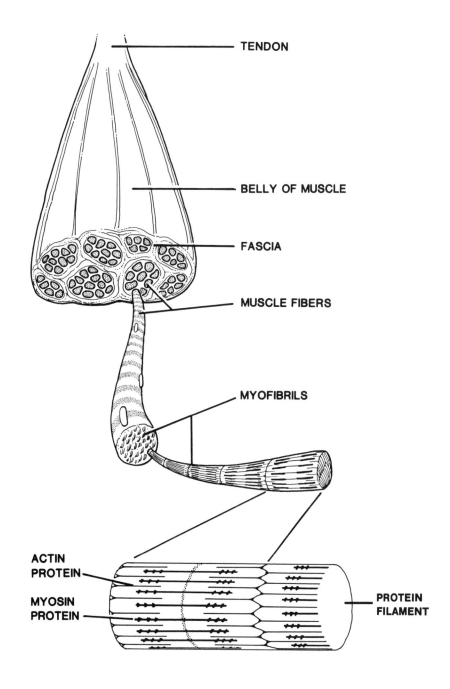

**Figure 10.4.** *Cross-sectional view of muscle. Notice that it is compartmentalized into smaller units or bundles.*

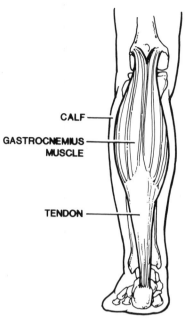

CALF

GASTROCNEMIUS
MUSCLE

TENDON

**Figure 10.5.** *A muscle with its tendons. Tendons attach a muscle to the skeletal system and are a compilation of all of the connective tissue surrounding all of the various fibers and bundles within the muscle.*

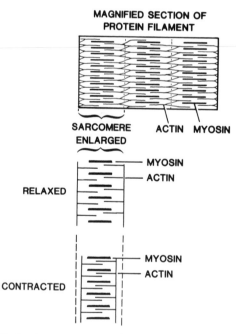

MAGNIFIED SECTION OF
PROTEIN FILAMENT

SARCOMERE    ACTIN   MYOSIN
ENLARGED

RELAXED          MYOSIN
                 ACTIN

CONTRACTED       MYOSIN
                 ACTIN

**Figure 10.6.** *The magnification of a sarcomere at rest and contracted. Notice how the thicker protein, myosin, pulls actin in toward the middle of the sarcomere.*

## SECTION OF PROTEIN FILAMENT MAGNIFIED

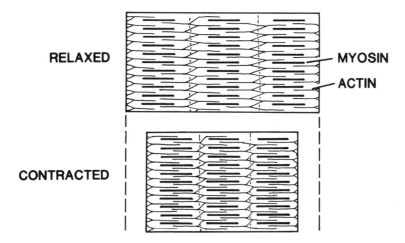

**Figure 10.7.** *A section of a protein filament showing how all of the sarcomeres within it contract to shorten the fiber.*

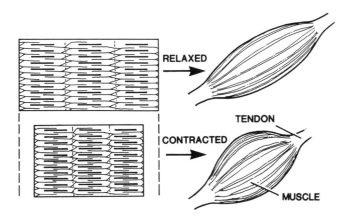

**Figure 10.8.** *Diagram of a muscle showing how the sarcomeres are situated in it and how they shorten to exert a pull on both tendons.*

---

A bundle of muscle fibers is called a _____ (FASCICULUS, MUSCLE CELL).

FASCICULUS

Another name for a muscle cell is a muscle _____ . (FIBER, FASCICULUS, FILAMENT)

MUSCLE FIBER

A muscle fiber is composed of _____ (MYOFIBRILS, FASCICULI).

MYOFIBRILS

A myofibril is composed of many _____ filaments arranged in rows.

PROTEIN

A _____ (MYOFIBRIL, SARCOMERE) is the smallest contractile unit in a muscle fiber.

SARCOMERE

A _____ (FASCICULUS, MUSCLE FIBER) has the thickness of a human hair.

MUSCLE FIBER

Muscle tissue is composed of the structural proteins _____ and _____ .

ACTIN, MYOSIN

_____ (ACTIN, MYOSIN) is the thicker protein structure found in the middle of the sarcomere.

MYOSIN

When a muscle receives an impulse from the nervous system, _____ (ACTIN, MYOSIN) will pull _____ (AC-TIN, MYOSIN) in towards the center of the sarcomere, thus reducing its border.

MYOSIN, ACTIN

The most widely accepted theory of muscle contraction is called the _____ _____ .

SLIDING FILAMENT

---

## Generating Force

It is important to understand that the interaction of actin and myosin sliding past each other is responsible for generating the force that the muscle is able to exert. As the borders of the sarcomeres shorten, the muscle fiber also shortens, which exerts a pull on the tendons that are attached to the skeletal system. This results in movement because the force, which is generated in the sarcomeres, is transmitted through the tendons to the skeletal system. If you can recall from Chapter 8, the more motor units that are activated at one time, the greater the force produced by the muscle. Obviously, with more motor units firing, you also have more muscle fibers contracting at one time. And, of course, since the muscle fiber is actually composed of millions of sarcomeres, it is really their simultaneous shortening that produces the greater force in the muscle.

## Large Muscle Force Capacity

A larger muscle is, generally speaking, a stronger one simply because it has more sarcomeres that can shorten to generate force. There are always going to be extenuating circumstances where this may not hold true, but, for the most part, larger muscles usu-ally mean greater strength. In the same regard, men are generally stronger than women simply because they have greater muscle mass. The hormone testosterone is responsible for this increase in muscle size in the male. There is absolutely *no difference* in the *quality* of muscle tissue between the sexes. The ability of male and female muscle tissue to generate force is exactly the same. It is just that *men* have *more* muscle tissue.

## MUSCLE HYPERTROPHY

The most accepted theory to date on muscle hypertrophy takes the position that the individual muscle fibers or cells *increase* in *size* and not number. Although there has been recent research showing some muscle fibers splitting or increasing in number, there still needs to be much more corroborating work done before this theory can be accepted. In Figure 10.9, you can see there is an increase in the protein filaments contained within the myofibril. This increase in protein is accomplished by adding more sarcomeres and rows of sarcomeres to the myofibrils. Of course, this will result in the myofibril increasing in size, which will also increase the size of the individual muscle fiber. Since this phenomenon is occurring in other fibers throughout the muscle, the result is that the entire muscle will increase in size. It is important to remember that this whole process is essentially adding actin and myosin proteins in a very specific structural pattern to the existing fibers within the muscle.

## MUSCLE ATROPHY

If protein filaments (sarcomeres) can be added to a muscle with training, these same filaments can be taken away or absorbed by the body with disuse or inactivity. This phenomenon is referred to as atrophy or the wasting away of muscle tissue. Whenever there is a period of immobilization, disuse or inactivity, muscle atrophy will occur to some extent. The more prolonged the inactivity and immobilization, the more pronounced the atrophy that occurs. It is important to keep in mind that the muscle fibers or cells are still present and do not disappear. It is only the protein contained within each fiber that is reduced. Thus, protein filaments can be added or taken away from a muscle fiber depending upon the amount of activity or lack of stimulation that it receives.

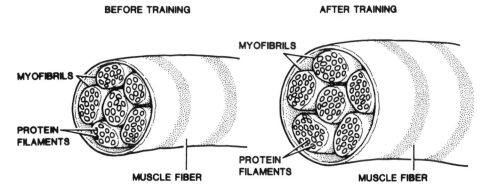

**Figure 10.9.** *Diagram showing how muscle hypertrophies. Notice there is an increase in protein filaments (rows of sarcomeres) within each myofibril that increases the size of the muscle fiber.*

## Benefit of Weight Training Through the Years

It is important to exercise all of your life in order to minimize or diminish the effects that inactivity has on the body. With aging and lack of use, muscle fibers have a tendency to lose protein filaments. Unfortunately, the body operates in such a way that abilities that are not utilized are lost. You do not, however, have to accept significant loses of strength or muscle function with age. With a consistent, yet modest, weight training program, you can maintain excellent muscle strength, tone and definition throughout your lifetime.

## Training for Muscle Hypertrophy

In Chapter 2, we talked about the specificity principle, which simply stated that the body responds in a very specific manner to the type of demands or training placed upon it. When you train with heavy resistances and few repetitions (one to 10), in essence you are asking or demanding from your body greater strength. The body responds by adding rows of sarcomeres to existing muscle fibers, one of the only means it has to increase

**Figure 10.10.** *The use of heavy resistances had to be a part of this athlete's training program in order to obtain the oustanding muscle development demonstrated in this photo.*

strength. So, one of the results of lifting heavy resistances is an increase in muscle size (primarily in men), which will contribute to an increase in muscle strength. If you were to train with light weights and more repetitions, however, this adaptation in the muscle would not occur. Since you are not asking or demanding that your body become stronger but that it become more efficient at reducing fatigue, muscle will not respond to this type of training by adding more protein filaments.

## MUSCLE FIBER TYPING

Researchers have identified several types of muscle fibers and categorized them according to their contractile characteristics. Fast twitch muscle fibers have large motor nerves, contract very quickly, are recruited for intense activity and fatigue rapidly. There are two sub-categories of fast twitch fibers based on their ability to resist fatigue. Slow twitch muscle fibers, on the other hand, have smaller motor nerves, contract slower, are recruited for mild activities and resist fatigue. Endurance athletes have a very large proportion of slow twitch fibers in their leg muscles (80 percent or more) compared to the average individual (50 percent slow twitch). Sprinters, on the other hand, have a slightly higher proportion of fast twitch fibers in their legs (60 to 70 percent). At one time, fiber typing was thought to be the key to discovering young talent and developing them into Olympic champions. Subsequent research, however, has shown that muscle fiber type is only one component of a profile necessary to be a successful international athlete. It takes much more than the right fiber type to make it to the top.

---

It is the shortening of the _____ (SARCOMERES, MYOFIBRILS) that allows the muscle to generate force.

SARCOMERES

Generally speaking, larger muscles _____ (ARE, ARE NOT) generally able to exert more force than smaller muscles.

ARE

Larger muscles have more _____ than smaller muscles that can shorten to generate force.

SARCOMERES/PROTEIN FILAMENTS

The quality of muscle tissue between the sexes is the _____ (SAME, DIFFERENT).

SAME

Men are generally stronger than women because they have _____ (SUPERIOR, MORE) muscle tissue.

MORE

The dominant male hormone responsible for enhancing the synthesis of new muscle tissue is _____ (ESTROGEN, TESTOSTERONE).

TESTOSTERONE

The increase in muscle size is referred to as _____ (HYPERTROPHY, ATROPHY).

HYPERTROPHY

With the most accepted theory to date, the individual fibers within a muscle increase in _____(SIZE, NUMBER) and not _____ (SIZE, NUMBER) in response to a weight training program.

SIZE, NUMBER

If a muscle increases in size from a weight training program, it will, in all probability, be a _____ muscle since it will have more sarcomeres to generate force.

STRONGER

With inactivity, disuse or immobilization, a muscle will decrease in size. This is referred to as _____ (ATROPHY, HYPERTROPHY).

ATROPHY

With atrophy, the _____ (MUSCLE FIBERS, PROTEIN FILAMENTS) are absorbed back into the body.

PROTEIN FILAMENTS

It is important to exercise your muscles throughout your lifetime in order to help minimize the _____ of muscle tissue through inactivity and disuse.

LOSS

To initiate the growth of new muscle tissue, it is necessary to lift (HEAVY, LIGHT) _____ weights and (FEW, MANY) _____ repetitions.

HEAVY, FEW

Lifting light weights and many repetitions _____ (WILL, WILL NOT) enhance muscle hypertrophy since you are demanding something other than strength from your muscles.

WILL NOT

Which fiber type (FAST, SLOW) is used in intense activity?

FAST

Which fiber type (FAST, SLOW) has large motor nerves but fatigues easily?

FAST

Which fiber type (FAST, SLOW) would be used in long distance running?

SLOW

Which fiber type (FAST, SLOW) has smaller motor nerves and is used in mild activities?

SLOW

# 11

# Nutrition for Energy Production

Most students participating in weight training classes are extremely interested in learning about nutrition. They are acutely aware that building large, defined muscles involves not only work in the weight room but proper choices at the dinner table. Basic to an understanding of nutrition is an understanding of the concepts of both aerobic and anaerobic metabolism. Why is this important? Because the *foods* that you *consume* are used or *metabolized* by the body for energy production, growth and maintenance. If you understand what nutrients are used for what purposes, you will have a much better understanding of what foods you need to consume for energy production or the building of muscle tissue. This chapter concerns nutrition as it relates to energy production for muscular effort. In the next chapter, we will discuss how nutrition contributes to an increase in muscle size.

It is important to realize that it takes energy for the actin and myosin filaments that we talked about in Chapter 10 to slide past each other to generate force. Without the body producing this energy, there would be no way for us to move or contract our muscles. Muscle cells have only a limited amount of stored energy. Consequently, they must continually resupply or renew their energy source if the muscle is to continue doing repeated contractions or work.

## METABOLISM

Metabolism can be defined, for the purposes of this book, as the breakdown and use of nutrients by the body for growth, maintenance and energy for muscular effort. Of the six nutrients (carbohydrates, fats, proteins, vitamins, minerals and water), only carbohydrates, fats and proteins are used by the body to produce the energy needed for muscle contractions (Figure 11.1). Vitamins and minerals assist in the breaking down or metabolism of the three nutrients (carbohydrates, fats and proteins) to produce energy but produce no energy themselves.

The body relies almost exclusively on fats and carbohydrates to produce energy for muscular effort (Figure 11.2). Eighty-five to 90 percent of the energy that you use to move your muscles comes from these two sources. The other 10 to 15 percent comes from the breakdown or metabolism of proteins. Proteins are primarily used by the body for biochemical reactions plus growth and repair of tissue, not energy production. Consequently, if you want energy for a workout or for an athletic event, it is important to realize that most of it is comes from carbohydrates and fats, not from proteins.

## SIX NUTRIENTS

Carbohydrates ⎫
Fats           ⎬ Provide energy for
Proteins       ⎭ muscular effort

Vitamins
Minerals
Water

**Figure 11.1.** *A list of the six nutrients, three of which contribute energy for muscular effort.*

## PRIMARY SOURCES OF ENERGY FOR MUSCULAR EFFORT

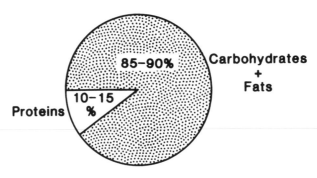

**Figure 11.2.** *The percentage of energy that each nutrient contributes to muscular effort. Notice that carbohydrates and fats contribute the greatest percentage of energy for aerobic activity.*

## AEROBIC AND ANAEROBIC METABOLISM

Weight training is considered an anaerobic activity, which means that the energy needed for muscular effort is produced with an inadequate supply of oxygen in the cell. In contrast, aerobic metabolism produces energy from the breakdown of nutrients with adequate amounts of oxygen present in the cell. Aerobic exercises are characterized by rhythmical, low-intensity, longer-duration activities. Jogging, swimming, bicycling, hiking, etc., are examples of activities that utilize aerobic metabolism for energy production. Anaerobic exercises, on the other hand, are characterized by high-intensity, shorter-duration activities. Sprinting, fast-break basketball, weight training, or an intense point in tennis or racquetball would all be considered anaerobic activities. It is important to realize, however, that even the aerobic activities identified above can become anaerobic if the intensity is such that oxygen cannot be delivered to the cell rapidly enough. Consequently, it depends upon the *intensity* of *effort* rather than the type of *activity* that determines whether the energy needed for muscular effort will be produced aerobically or anaerobically.

## Carbohydrates and Anaerobic Metabolism

The only nutrient that can be broken down to produce energy anaerobically are carbohydrates (breads, pasta, rice, beans, sugars, etc.). Fats and proteins cannot be metabolized anaerobically, consequently, consuming them before any high-intensity activity or effort would not be productive. Since *weight training* is considered an *anaerobic* activity, consuming anything but carbohydrates prior to a workout would not provide you with the energy you would be seeking. However, carbohydrates and fats, as well as proteins to a much lesser extent, can be utilized or metabolized by the body aerobically to produce energy for muscular effort.

---

Basic to an understanding of nutrition is a need to understand _____.

### METABOLISM

Metabolism is the way the body breaks down nutrients and uses them to produce _____ for muscular effort, growth and maintenance of body tissues.

### ENERGY

Of the six nutrients, which three can be used by the body to produce energy for muscle contractions?

### CARBOHYDRATES, FATS, PROTEINS

Of the three nutrients identified above, which two are primarily used (85% of the time) for energy to produce muscle contractions aerobically?

### FATS, CARBOHYDRATES

Which of the nutrients is primarily used by the body for growth and maintenance purposes only?

### PROTEINS

Vitamins _____ in the breaking down of nutrients to produce energy but do not directly contribute to energy for muscle contractions themselves.

### ASSIST

In _____ (ANAEROBIC, AEROBIC) metabolism, nutrients are broken down in the absence of adequate amounts of oxygen to produce energy for muscular effort.

### ANAEROBIC

In aerobic metabolism, nutrients are broken down in the _____ (ABSENCE, PRESENCE) of adequate amounts of oxygen to produce energy for muscular effort.

### PRESENCE

Weight training is considered an (AEROBIC, ANAEROBIC) activity.

ANAEROBIC

What nutrient is the only source of energy used for muscle contractions during anaerobic activity?

CARBOHYDRATES

What nutrients can be utilized to produce energy for muscular effort aerobically?

CARBOHYDRATES, FATS, PROTEINS

## ATP—ENERGY FOR MUSCLE CONTRACTION

It is important to understand that the nutrients we consume are not a direct but rather an indirect source of energy for muscle contractions. The only source of energy for muscle contractions comes from the breakdown of adenosine triphosphate, commonly referred to as ATP (Figure 11.3). When a muscle receives an electrical impulse from the

$$ATP \rightleftharpoons ADP + P + Energy \uparrow$$
$$Adenosine \sim P \sim P \sim P \rightarrow Adenosine \sim P \sim P \quad + P + Energy \uparrow$$
$$ATP \leftarrow Adenosine \sim P \sim P + P + Energy \text{ From Nutrients}$$

**Figure 11.3.** *The breakdown of adenosine triphosphate (ATP) in the muscle is the only source of energy for muscular effort. The energy in food is used to resynthesize more ATP so the muscle can continue to contract.*

nervous system, ATP is broken down into its subsequent components and releases energy in the process. It is this release of energy that allows the protein filaments to slide past each other, resulting in a muscle contraction. If there is no ATP present in the muscle, it cannot contract. Unfortunately, there is only enough ATP available in the cell to last for a few seconds worth of activity. Consequently, after that point, ATP has to continually be resynthesized or resupplied in order for the muscle to continue contracting.

Notice in Figure 11.3 that the ATP reaction is a reversible one. Energy will be needed to resynthesize or reattach the free phosphate atom to the ADP (adenosine diphosphate) molecule to form ATP again. That energy comes from the energy stored in the nutrients that we consume. Consequently, food represents an indirect rather than direct source of energy for muscle contractions. The energy released from the breakdown of the nutrients is used by the muscle to resynthesize ADP into ATP. This process allows muscle to contract an unlimited number of times as long as there is enough energy present from the nutrients. Whenever the supply of nutrients is used up, the muscle will no longer be able to reconvert ADP into ATP. Consequently, fatigue and exhaustion will set in and muscle contractions will cease.

Food is a/an _____ (DIRECT, INDIRECT) source of energy for muscle contractions.

INDIRECT

The energy needed for a muscle contraction comes from the breakdown of what molecule?

ADENOSINE TRIPHOSPHATE (ATP)

There is a/an _____ (LIMITED, UNLIMITED) supply of ATP available in the muscle cell.

LIMITED

If there is no ATP present in the muscle, it _____ (WILL HAVE, WILL NOT HAVE) the ability to contract.

WILL NOT HAVE

What is released when ATP is broken down into its smaller components?

ENERGY

When ATP is being resynthesized from ADP and free phosphate, what is needed?

ENERGY

Where does that energy to resynthesize ATP come from?

NUTRIENTS

## Intensity Factor

It is important to realize that energy can be produced both aerobically and anaerobically at the same time. The more intense the effort, the greater the contribution that comes from anaerobic sources. The less intense the effort, the greater the aerobic contribution. Figure 11.4 addresses the contributions of each type of metabolism from sprinting to running a marathon. As you can see, a mile run utilizes 50 percent of each type of metabolism.

In light intensity activity, the body has enough time to take in oxygen and deliver it to the working muscle where it combines with nutrients, providing the energy necessary to continue resynthesizing ATP. However, as the intensity of activity starts to increase, it becomes exceedingly more difficult for oxygen to reach the cell in time to assist in this process. Consequently, some of the energy to resynthesize ATP will now be produced anaerobically as well as aerobically. If the intensity of effort continues to accelerate, anaerobic metabolism will continue contributing a greater share of energy production as aerobic metabolism begins shutting down.

Muscle has only a limited ability to produce energy anaerobically (40 to 60 seconds of all-out activity). Aerobic metabolism, on the other hand, can be continued indefinitely as long as the supply of nutrients lasts. If muscle cells did not have the capacity to produce

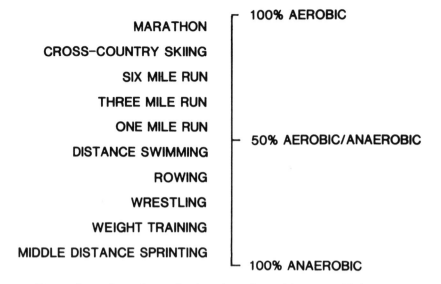

MARATHON ⎡ 100% AEROBIC
CROSS-COUNTRY SKIING
SIX MILE RUN
THREE MILE RUN
ONE MILE RUN
DISTANCE SWIMMING ⊢ 50% AEROBIC/ANAEROBIC
ROWING
WRESTLING
WEIGHT TRAINING
MIDDLE DISTANCE SPRINTING ⎣ 100% ANAEROBIC

**Figure 11.4.** *Diagram showing the contributions of aerobic and anaerobic metabolism from middle distance sprints to the marathon. Notice that both types of metabolism can be going on at the same time. However, as intensity increases, a greater proportion of the energy comes from anaerobic metabolism.*

energy without oxygen, there would be no way for us to do any type of activity requiring an intense effort for more than a few seconds. Fortunately, there are mechanisms in the cell that allow us to produce a limited amount of energy anaerobically but not without suffering the consequences of that metabolism.

## ANAEROBIC METABOLISM AND LACTIC ACID

Referring to Figure 11.5, you can see that the end products of aerobic metabolism for a molecule of glucose are $CO_2$ and $H_2O$, both relatively easy by-products to dispose of in the body ($CO_2$ through respiration, $H_2O$ through sweat, respiration and urination). However, the end product of anaerobic metabolism, lactic acid, creates a different sort of

---

### CARBOHYDRATE METABOLISM

Carbohydrate → Glucose + $O_2$ → $CO_2$ + $H_2O$ (Aerobic Metabolism)

Carbohydrate → Glucose + $NoO_2$ → Lactic Acid (Anaerobic Metabolism)

---

**Figure 11.5.** *The end products of aerobic and anaerobic metabolism of a molecule of glucose. The rapid accumulation of lactic acid from anaerobic metabolism can cause a burning sensation in the muscle.*

problem. Lactic acid accumulates in the cell and surrounding tissue and is the substance that causes pain during intense muscular contractions. If enough lactic acid accumulates in the muscle rapidly, it will eventually necessitate cessation of activity. It is easy to experience lactic acid accumulation in the muscle simply by lifting a submaximal resistance until fatigue or exhaustion. The burning feeling you experience in your muscles is the accumulation of lactic acid. A brief rest period, however, will allow the lactic acid to dissipate in the muscle and surrounding tissue so that subsequent activity can be continued.

## Muscle Soreness

It is important to realize that the pain you experience from lactic acid accumulation is not injuring the muscle. Once you stop exercising, the pain should disappear within 30 to 60 seconds. Although many people believe lactic acid is the problem, the soreness that accompanies intense muscular activity in the following day(s) is not caused by lactic acid accumulation. Lactic acid levels return to normal resting values within a few hours. Consequently, it is highly unlikely for lactic acid to be the cause of muscle soreness after an intense effort since it is no longer present in the muscle.

---

Identify the two types of metabolism, _____ with oxygen and _____ without oxygen.

AEROBIC, ANAEROBIC

Which type of metabolism is associated with high-intensity, short-duration activity?

ANAEROBIC

Which type of metabolism is associated with low-intensity, long-duration activity?

AEROBIC

What type of energy system does weight training utilize?

ANAEROBIC

The metabolism that provides energy for the resynthesis of ATP without oxygen being present is called _____ .

ANAEROBIC METABOLISM

Muscle has a/an _____ (LIMITED, UNLIMITED) ability to produce energy anaerobically.

LIMITED

We have the ability to produce energy anaerobically (all-out effort) for approximately _____ to _____ seconds.

40, 60

The end products of aerobic metabolism for a molecule of glucose are _____ and _____ .

$CO_2$ AND $H_2O$

The end product of anaerobic metabolism for a molecule of glucose is _____ .

LACTIC ACID

The rapid onset of pain that accompanies intense muscular contractions is caused by the accumulation of _____

LACTIC ACID

The soreness in muscles in the day(s) following intense muscular contractions _____(IS, IS NOT) caused by the accumulation of lactic acid in the muscle.

IS NOT

High lactic acid levels after intense muscular contractions return to normal resting levels in a relatively _____ (SHORT, LONG) period of time after exercise.

SHORT

## Nutrients and Metabolism

Throughout the chapter, we have been talking about how the various nutrients contribute the energy contained within their structures to resynthesize ATP either aerobically or anaerobically. Now, however, it is time to take a closer look to see what happens to each nutrient once it enters the cell.

As you look at Figure 11.6, you can see that the muscle cell contains rows and rows of protein filaments that makes it unique from any other cell in the body. In addition to the protein filaments, notice also the oval-shaped mitochondria, which are referred to as the energy storehouse of the cell. They play a significant role in the process of ATP resynthesis.

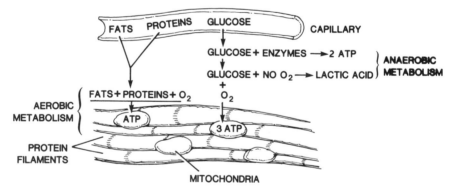

**Figure 11.6.** *Diagram of a muscle cell showing how it metabolizes glucose (carbohydrates), fats, and proteins. Notice that the only nutrient that can provide energy to resynthesize ATP anaerobically is glucose. All three nutrients, however, can provide energy for ATP resynthesis aerobically in the mitochondria of the cell.*

## CARBOHYDRATE METABOLISM

As you can see in Figure 11.6, the bloodstream delivers carbohydrates (now broken down to its smallest component, glucose), fats, and proteins to the muscle cell. Immediately upon entering the cell, the glucose molecule is acted upon by *enzymes* in the watery medium of the cell (called the sarcoplasm). The net result is the *resynthesis* of *two* ATP molecules. This reaction occurs whether oxygen is present in the cell or not, so, in essence, what has just been described is the process of *anaerobic* metabolism. Notice that there are no enzymes present in the cell to break down fats and proteins without oxygen being present. Consequently, these two nutrients cannot participate in anaerobic metabolism.

After glucose has been broken down to produce two ATP molecules anaerobically, whether it continues to be broken down further to release its energy depends upon the availability of oxygen. If *adequate* amounts of oxygen are present in the cell, the glucose molecule (now converted to pyruvate) enters the *mitochondria*, where it is broken down still further to produce 36 ATP molecules. The process just described is *aerobic* metabolism. If, due to the intensity of exercise, there are inadequate amounts of oxygen present in the cell, the glucose molecule cannot enter the mitochondria but is converted into lactic acid. Thus, the end product of anaerobic metabolism is lactic acid.

## FAT AND PROTEIN METABOLISM

Notice the only place that *fats* and *proteins* can contribute to the resynthesis of ATP production is in the *mitochondria* of the cell. Consequently, they can only be involved in energy production *aerobically* since nothing can be carried into the mitochondria without adequate amounts of oxygen being present in the cell. Thus, the muscle cell has the capability to metabolize all *three* nutrients *aerobically* but only one nutrient, *carbohydrate*, *anaerobically*.

It is obvious that, in terms of carbohydrate metabolism, aerobic metabolism is 18 times more efficient or productive (36 to 2) than anaerobic metabolism. The more ATP being resynthesized in the cell, the greater the ability of the muscle to do repeated contractions without fatigue.

### Implications for Weight Training

In terms of nutrition, you hopefully now have a much better understanding of why carbohydrates, and not protein or fat, are the only nutrients that can provide energy for intense muscular activity. If you want energy for your weight workout, you will not get it from proteins. There is no mechanism in the cell that can release the energy contained in the protein molecules without the presence of adequate amounts of oxygen in the cell. Consequently, carbohydrates should be your pre-workout food of choice for the energy you desire during your workout.

# THE PRE-EVENT MEAL

Most nutritionists recommend that the pre-event meal should be light, consumed at least three hours prior to competition and consist mostly of carbohydrates since they will be used almost exclusively in any type of high-intensity activity. Carbohydrates are also easily digested in comparison to fats and proteins. If the nutrients you consume are not in the bloodstream prior to competition, they will not be able to contribute to energy production. Therefore, there is little benefit to consuming anything that is not digested before a contest.

It is important that an athlete consume food to which his digestive system is accustomed. Anything that the body is not used to digesting may cause gastric problems that could inhibit athletic performance. Outside these few guidelines, there is not much more to say about a pre-event meal. There is no "super meal" that will enhance an athlete's performance. What he consumes, however, can influence his performance by preventing a maximal effort. Remember, nutrition is only one part of the athlete's total preparation for a contest. It can never compensate for an athlete's lack of skill, conditioning, or preparation.

---

Most carbohydrates are broken down to what before being utilized by the body for energy?

GLUCOSE

Anaerobic metabolism produces _____ (1, 2, 3, 4) molecules of ATP for every molecule of glucose that is broken down.

2

What is the only nutrient (carbohydrate, fat, protein) that can be broken down anaerobically to resynthesize ATP?

CARBOHYDRATES

Anaerobic metabolism can break down nutrients to resynthesize ATP in the absence of adequate amounts of _____ .

OXYGEN

A lack of _____ results in fats and proteins being unable to be metabolized anaerobically for ATP resynthesis.

ENZYMES

Taking extra protein _____ (WILL, WILL NOT) give you extra energy for a weight training workout.

WILL NOT

Whether or not glucose (converted to pyruvate now) will continue in aerobic metabolism or be converted into lactic acid is determined by _____ .

PRESENCE OF OXYGEN IN THE CELL

If there is an insufficient amount of oxygen present in the cell, glucose will form _____ .

LACTIC ACID

If there is a sufficient amount of oxygen present in the cell, glucose (pyruvate) will enter the _____ and produce _____ (20, 30, 36, 40) ATP.

MITOCHONDRIA, 36

Fats and proteins can only be metabolized in the _____ .

MITOCHONDRIA

Which energy system (AEROBIC, ANAEROBIC) is more efficient in producing or resynthesizing ATP?

AEROBIC

The pre-event meal should be light and consist primarily of what nutrient?

CARBOHYDRATES

Nutrition is only one _____ of an athlete's total preparation for an athletic contest.

PART OR FACTOR

Nutrition _____ (CAN, CANNOT) make up for lack of training or preparation for a given contest.

CANNOT

# 12

# Nutrition for Muscle Growth

In Chapter 11, we discussed in some detail how nutrients are used by the body to produce energy for muscular effort. Now, it is time to focus on how nutrients contribute to muscle growth. Since muscle is composed of protein (actin and myosin), there seems to be some ambiguity surrounding how much protein is needed to encourage and enhance muscle hypertrophy. If some protein is necessary for muscle growth (which it is), is more better? And how much is enough? Where do the benefits of extra protein consumption start to drop off? Hopefully, the information presented in this chapter will help resolve some of these issues.

## THE MAKEUP OF CARBOHYDRATES, FATS, AND PROTEINS

All of these nutrients are composed of the same atoms: carbon, hydrogen and oxygen. The distinguishing feature between carbohydrates, fats and proteins is simply the number and arrangement of these atoms. Fats have more carbon and hydrogen but fewer oxygen atoms than carbohydrates (Figure 12.1). Proteins differ from carbohydrates and fats in that they have nitrogen and, in some cases, sulfur atoms. Consequently, depending upon what is needed at the time, the body can reconstruct any of these nutrients (since they all contain the same atoms) into a carbohydrate (glucose) for energy, a fat for storage, or a protein for muscle tissue. The priorities of the body, however, are (1) energy, (2) synthesizing of new muscle tissue, and (3) storage of calories as fat. If the first two priorities are met, the body will convert any extra calories, unfortunately, into fat.

## AMINO ACIDS—BUILDING BLOCKS OF ALL PROTEINS

The building blocks of all proteins are substances called amino acids. There are 22 different amino acids. *Fourteen* can be synthesized in the body from carbohydrates and fats in the diet. Consequently, they are referred to as *non-essential* amino acids. *Eight* amino acids must be consumed from protein sources in the diet, thus they are referred to as *essential* amino acids.

Proteins are extremely complex molecules consisting of long chains of amino acids. If you think of the 22 amino acids as letters in the alphabet, you get some idea of how many different proteins can be created by combining amino acids in different arrangements. The body literally contains hundreds of different proteins from muscle tissue to complex enzymes, hormones and blood components. Many of these proteins contain hundreds of amino acids combined together in a specific sequence or pattern. If any key amino acids

Glucose (Carbohydrate)

$$C_6H_{12}O_6$$

Palmitic Acid (Fat)

$$CH_3(CH_2)_{14}COOH$$

**Figure 12.1.** *The molecular formulas for a molecule of fat and carbohydrate. Notice that the only difference lies in the number of carbon, hydrogen and oxygen atoms. Fats have more carbon (16-to-6) and hydrogen (32-to-12) but fewer oxygen atoms (2-to-6) than a carbohydrate.*

are missing when the body is trying to synthesize a specific protein, the process will stop until all of those necessary to construct the protein are available.

The most complete sources of essential amino acids in the diet are eggs, meat and dairy products. Certain vegetables are also good sources; however, they may lack one or two essential amino acids. Consequently, vegetarians must be careful when planning their meals to ensure they are getting all of the essential amino acids in their diets. By combining certain foods such as rice and beans in a meal, this problem can be solved quite easily.

## PROTEIN CONSUMPTION

Generally speaking, it is recommended that you consume in grams of protein each day approximately what your body weight is in kilograms (Figure 12.2). Since it takes approximately 29 grams to equal an ounce, you can see that it does not take a lot of protein to meet your daily requirements. Most sports nutritionists support the position that athletes engaged in strenuous activities should consume slightly greater amounts of protein each day. Protein consumption should be increased in grams to somewhere from 1.6 to 2.5 times the body weight in kilograms. As you can see from Figure 12.2, even this amount of protein is not very much.

Many weightlifters and body builders consume 10 to 20 times these recommended levels on a daily basis. Although these athletes may believe this extra consumption helps them build muscle tissue faster, whatever is not used for that purpose or for energy production will end up as fat. Consuming more protein in the diet may have little impact on the rate of muscle synthesis in the cell. The fact that these individuals happen to be building larger muscles may have far less to do with their excess protein consumption than with the amount of effort they are putting forth in their workouts. It is easy, however, for them to erroneously attribute their increase in muscle size to the extra protein they are consuming rather than to the hard workouts.

## CALCULATION FOR DAILY PROTEIN

Body weight in pounds ÷ 2.2 = Body weight in kilograms

Example: 150 lbs ÷ 2.2 = 68.2 kilograms

Need to consume 68.2 grams/protein/day or
2.3 ounces of protein (68.2 ÷ 29 = 2.3 ounces)

## PROTEIN CONSUMPTION FOR HEAVY EXERCISE

68.2 grams × 2.5 = 170 grams/protein/day

170 ÷ 29 grams = 6 ounces protein/day

Note: 1 ounce = 29 grams, approximately

**Figure 12.2.** *Illustration showing how to calculate daily protein consumption.*

Carbohydrates, fats and proteins can all be reconstructed for whatever needs the body has because they all contain these same atoms: _____ , _____ , and _____ .

CARBON, HYDROGEN, OXYGEN

Proteins differ from fats and carbohydrates in that they not only contain carbon, hydrogen and oxygen atoms but also _____ and sometimes _____ .

NITROGEN, SULFUR

The priorities of the body's need for nutrients are first, _____ production, second, _____ of new muscle tissue and third, _____ as _____ .

ENERGY, SYNTHESIS, STORAGE, FAT

After the first two priorities are met, any excess calories will be converted into _____ .

FAT

The building blocks of all proteins are the 22 _____ _____ .

AMINO ACIDS

The 22 amino acids are like the letters of the alphabet in that there are endless combinations possible. The more complex proteins in the body contain _____ of amino acids combined together.

HUNDREDS

"Essential" amino acids means that they _____ (HAVE TO, DO NOT HAVE TO) be taken in by the diet since the body cannot manufacture them from other nutrients.

HAVE TO

The 14 non-essential amino acids can be synthesized from what nutrients in the diet?

CARBOHYDRATES, FATS

The most complete source of essential amino acids in the diet comes from what foods, meat and dairy products or vegetables?

MEAT AND DAIRY PRODUCTS

The quantity of protein you should consume each day in grams is equal to your body weight in _____ .

KILOGRAMS

Athletes engaged in strenuous muscular activity could possibly consume in grams of protein each day approximately _____ to _____ times their body weight in kilograms.

1.6 to 2.5

Athletes who consume inordinate amounts of protein do so with the intention of _____ the rate of muscle synthesis or growth.

ENHANCING OR ACCELERATING

---

# AMINO ACID PILLS

With competitive lifters, a new trend has evolved over the past several years that involves taking of amino acid pills. Since the protein is already broken down into its subsequent components (amino acids), athletes believe that it will get into their systems more quickly, enhancing the synthesis of new muscle tissue. Many weightlifters also insist that taking amino acids prior to their workout gives them more energy during their workout. As you have learned from the preceding chapter, however, proteins cannot be broken down to produce energy anaerobically. Whether it is in the form of protein consumed in the diet or amino acid pills, extra protein represents extra calories, and the body will respond according to its priorities: energy, muscle synthesis and fat storage.

## Protein-Sparing Effects of Carbohydrates and Fats

The body's first priority for nutrients is energy production since that ensures the survival of the individual. If the diet is insufficient in providing this energy from fats and carbohydrates, the body will get it from proteins at the expense of muscle tissue. Consequently, you will be working against yourself if you are trying to build muscle tissue and not ingesting enough calories to meet your energy needs. If you ingest enough calories from carbohydrates and fats to satisfy the body's need for energy, it will tend to spare the protein in the muscle tissue from being broken down to provide that energy. You should, therefore, be able to realize an increase in muscle size from your training program.

**Figure 12.3.** *Standing next to your competition accentuates the obvious strengths and weaknesses of each athlete. The unbelievable lat development and trim waistline of the competitor on the right indicates that he not only trained hard in the gym, but that he also made the right choices with his diet.*

## Rapid Weight Loss—Loss of Protein

Whenever there is a rapid weight loss of more than two pounds per week due to a reduction in calories from the diet, there is a good probability that some of that loss is not only coming from fat deposits in the body but from muscle tissue as well. Since the dieter is primarily interested in losing fat and not muscle and since muscle tissue is metabolically active at rest (burns calories), it isn't really as advantageous to lose weight this way. Even though the scale may say that your diet is working, you are actually maintaining the same percentage of body fat that you had prior to the diet since you are losing lean body weight, or muscle tissue, as well. Gradual weight loss of only a couple of pounds per week ensures that most of that reduction is coming from fat stores and not muscle tissue.

## STEROIDS AND MUSCLE HYPERTROPHY

The ingestion of steroids to enhance muscle hypertrophy has become a fairly common practice among some groups of athletes during the past decade. Steroids are synthetic male hormones taken in either pill or injectable form that appear to be very effective in terms of enhancing muscle hypertrophy. Steroids work by sending signals to the muscle cell to enhance protein synthesis on one end while retarding protein degradation on the other. The net result is that the muscle will significantly increase in size. By taking steroids, you are obviously doing something to increase the rate of protein synthesis in the cell, which is much different than consuming extra protein to enhance this development. However, individuals taking steroids also have to work out very hard in the weight room to bring about the increase in muscle size they are seeking. Without the effort in the weight room, the muscle-hypertrophying effects of taking steroids are greatly minimized.

## The Risk of Steroid Use

It is important to understand that the use of steroids is very controversial and may involve some long-term health risks and consequences for the individual. Some heavy users of steroids have had problems with organ cancers as well as male reproductive difficulties. Unfortunately, steroid abuse has not been going on for that long a time so evidence is still being collected. Presently, steroids are banned in international and Olympic competition as well as in many professional and intercollegiate sports. In addition to the health risks of steroid usage, there is the question of ethics. Steroids may be providing some athletes with an unfair advantage over their competition.

## Vitamin and Mineral Supplementation

As indicated earlier in this chapter, vitamins and minerals cannot produce energy themselves but assist in the process of releasing the energy contained within the nutrients. Generally speaking, unless your eating habits are very poor, vitamin and mineral supplementation is unnecessary. The American diet is sufficient in vitamins and minerals to satisfy the body's needs for growth and energy production. If, however, you are convinced that you need vitamin supplementation, you are much safer with a multipurpose one. Some individuals have had serious problems ingesting megadoses of certain fat-soluble (A, D, E, K) and water-soluble ($B_6$) vitamins.

---

You _____ (CAN, CANNOT) accelerate the rate of protein synthesis in the muscle just by consuming more protein.

CANNOT

Amino acid pills do _____ (SOMETHING, NOTHING) to alter the rate of protein synthesis in the muscle but only add more protein to the diet.

NOTHING

If the diet is insufficient in providing energy from carbohydrates and fats, the body _____ (WILL, WILL NOT) get this energy from muscle tissue.

WILL

Whenever there is rapid weight loss, there is a good possibility that _____ tissue is being lost as well as fat.

MUSCLE

Losing muscle tissue as well as fat _____ (WILL, WILL NOT) reduce the dieter's percentage of body fat.

WILL NOT

Steroids are synthetic male _____ .

HORMONES

Steroids work by _____ the rate of protein synthesis in the muscle as well as _____ the rate of protein loss or degradation.

INCREASING, DECREASING

The practice of taking steroids _____ (DOES, DOES NOT) involve some possible long-term health consequences.

DOES

The American diet is _____ (sufficient, insufficient) in terms of providing adequate quantities of vitamins and minerals.

SUFFICIENT

---

1

# 13

# Warm-up, Stretching and Flexibility

Proper warm-up is critical in any activity that involves strenuous muscular effort. Fortunately, in weight training, you can warm-up as long as necessary before engaging in the more difficult parts of your workout. Therefore, with this activity, you have some control over the potential for developing muscle soreness or injury.

Stretching is simply the lengthening or elongating of a muscle. It is usually done prior to activity with the intent of both increasing the range of motion (ROM) about a joint (flexibility) and keeping the muscle limber. Although it is very difficult to prove scientifically, it is thought that stretching prior to an activity will help prevent injury and muscle soreness. Many people mistakenly believe that stretching, by itself, is a good warm-up exercise that adequately prepares the body for the more strenuous activity to follow. It should be incorporated with some type of activity that elevates body temperature, however, to be truly effective.

Warming up prior to activity simply makes a muscle more receptive to stretching without injury. Muscle injury or soreness usually occurs because the actin and myosin filaments in the muscle fibers (Chapter 10) are disrupted by being pulled apart. Consequently, it is the overstretching of a muscle or the lengthening of a muscle with tension (eccentric contraction) that is primarily responsible for this condition. If a muscle is warmed up properly, the chance of injury or soreness is minimized since the muscle is more likely to stretch than pull.

## PROPER WARM-UP ACTIVITIES

Anything you do prior to exercise that elevates the temperature in a muscle could be considered a suitable warm-up activity. As simple as this may sound, you can assume that your muscles have been sufficiently warmed up when you start to break a sweat during your pre-exercise routine (usually five to 10 minutes of activity). Stationary bicycling, rope jumping or jogging are all good warm-up activities that can be used prior to lifting. Another good warm-up technique is to mimic the activity you will be doing during your exercise session but at a lesser intensity. Fortunately, in weight training, you can always do exercises with lighter weights before proceeding to the more strenuous parts of your workout.

Stretching a muscle prior to activity has little effect on elevating the temperature in it. Consequently, it has little value as a warm-up activity unless combined with some other type of exercise that does elevate body temperature. If you are going to stretch, it makes more sense to do so after you have warmed up, since the muscles will then be more receptive to maintaining the stretch or length you have applied to them. It is also a good idea to stretch after exercising since the muscles, particularly in weight training, tend to tighten and shorten from the activity. Stretching at this point, with the muscles still warm from exercising, will help to maintain their normal resting length.

## TYPES OF FLEXIBILITY

There are basically two types of flexibility: static and dynamic. *Static* flexibility involves how much *ROM* there is about a particular joint and is what we commonly associate with flexibility. *Dynamic* flexibility, on the other hand, measures how much *resistance* to movement there is through the ROM of a particular joint. If there is greater resistance, it takes more energy to move the joint through its ROM and a greater possibility of injury exists.

The long-held position regarding static flexibility is that people with poor ROM about a joint are more prone to injury because of their lack of flexibility. There seems to be more widespread recognition today, however, that it is not static but rather dynamic flexibility that is important in terms of preventing muscle injury and soreness. There is even some concern now about hyperflexibility or excessive ROM, which at one time was not considered a problem. Consequently, less emphasis and importance is now placed on static flexibility. Regardless of your degree of flexibility, whenever you extend yourself beyond your capabilities, the end result could be muscle soreness or injury.

## FACTORS AFFECTING FLEXIBILITY

There are many factors that affect flexibility: age, sex, physical activity, and the tightness of the soft tissue structures of muscle. Due to genetics, some people are inherently more flexible than others. Considering the sexes, women tend to be much more flexible than their male counterparts at any age past puberty.

Although flexibility decreases with age in both sexes, people who are physically active appear to retain a greater degree of flexibility than those who are inactive. This may simply be a factor of active individuals moving their muscles through a full ROM in their exercise programs. You should be more concerned with how much ROM or flexibility you lose through the years rather than with how flexible or inflexible you may have been compared to someone else.

### Weight Training and Flexibility

Contrary to popular opinion, training with weights does not decrease flexibility and result in a muscle-bound physique. Actually, lifters have been found to exhibit excellent flexibility despite their large muscles. If some of them have shown a reduced ROM about a joint, it has been due more to the enormous muscle mass they have developed rather than any restriction in the ability of their muscles to stretch out fully. Consequently, you should not be concerned about becoming muscle-bound or losing flexibility as a result of your training program.

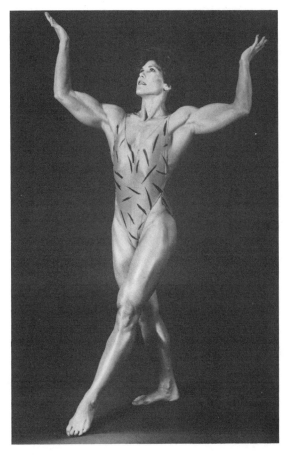

**Figure 13a.** *Sue Ann McKean, former winner of several amateur California body building titles, demonstrates style and grace with outstanding muscle development. She was a finalist in seven national amateur body building competitions, and she was the Amateur California Women's champion in 1983 and 1984.*

## Importance of Full ROM

Because you actually stretch as well as contract a muscle through the ROM in any lift, training with weights has the ability to actually enhance flexibility. It is important, however, that you use a full ROM when performing any lift. If you continually cut the ROM as shown in Figure 13.1, the muscle never gets stretched out. In time it can become tight or shortened, resulting in a decrease in ROM or flexibility. Unfortunately, it is usually easier to complete a lift if you don't bring the weight all the way back to its original resting position. Many beginning lifters have a tendency to fall into this habit. Discipline yourself to complete each lift with a full ROM to ensure that you are adequately stretching as well as contracting your muscles.

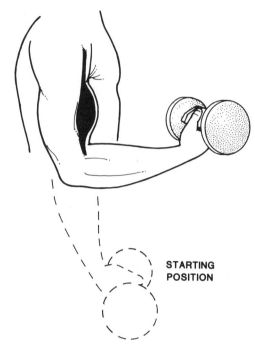

**STARTING POSITION**

**Figure 13.1.** *Illustration showing an incomplete range of motion for the bicep curl. Lifting like this could result in a decrease in flexibility of the bicep muscle.*

Stretching out and warming up _____ (ARE, ARE NOT) the same thing.

ARE NOT

Stretching out prior to an activity _____ (DOES, DOES NOT) constitute an adequate warm-up.

DOES NOT

A _____ (COLD, WARM) muscle is more responsive to being stretched without injury.

WARM

A proper warm-up involves any activity that _____ body or muscle temperature.

ELEVATES OR INCREASES

Name one exercise that is considered an adequate one to use as a warm-up.

JOGGING, STATIONARY BICYCLING, ROPE JUMPING

In many instances, muscle injury or soreness occurs when the muscle is _____ .

OVERSTRETCHED

Stretching a _____ (WARM, COLD) muscle will most likely result in the muscle retaining some of the stretch that you applied to it.

WARM

Prior to intense activity, it is much better to stretch _____ (BEFORE, AFTER) warming up.

AFTER

There is definitely _____ (SOME, NO) benefit to stretching after your workout.

SOME

A muscle that is never stretched becomes _____ .

TIGHT OR SHORTENED

The type of flexibility that involves how much ROM there is about a joint is called _____ (STATIC, DYNAMIC).

STATIC

The type of flexibility that involves the degree of resistance to movement through the ROM is called _____ (STATIC, DYNAMIC).

DYNAMIC

People who exhibit poor static flexibility (are inflexible) are _____ (MORE LIKELY, LESS LIKELY, NOT ANY MORE LIKELY) to get injured than people who exhibit good static flexibility.

NOT ANY MORE LIKELY

People who are active through the years retain _____ (MORE, LESS) flexibility than their inactive counterparts.

MORE

Weight training can actually _____ (INCREASE, DECREASE) one's flexibility if the exercises are done with a full ROM.

INCREASE

---

## STRETCHING CORRECTLY

It is important to understand the correct way to stretch in order to obtain the best results for your effort. The stretch should be slow and gradual, or, what we refer to as a static stretch. You should not stretch to the point of pain, nor should your muscles be pulling and straining. You should be relaxed, and there should be a mild stretch or tension in the muscles. After holding the initial stretch for approximately 15 to 30 seconds, you should try to increase the stretch a bit. You should find that the muscle is receptive to further stretching if you apply the tension in this manner. Continue to increase the stretch until you reach a point where further stretching would result in pain. Hold that position for 15 to 30 seconds.

Ballistic, or bouncing, movements are generally not encouraged when stretching. It is possible to overstretch the muscle this way and actually cause the muscle to contract or resist the stretch rather than relax and accept it. In addition, it is possible to elicit some muscle soreness by stretching in this manner.

## INJURY PREVENTION

Since you can control the intensity of your workout with weights, there is no reason why you should ever injure yourself from not warming up properly. Before you do any intense lifting, you should always make sure your muscles are warm by completing many sets at a lighter weight. If, for some reason, you can't get the tightness or soreness out of your muscles after doing a number of warm-up sets, then it would be advisable to reduce the intensity of your workout or to do more warm-up sets prior to getting into heavier lifting. To continue lifting through muscle tightness and soreness is really an invitation to further soreness and potential injury.

### Progressive Soreness

If you continue experiencing muscle soreness from week to week, try stretching out and warming up properly prior to lifting. You should also consider cutting back on the intensity of your workout for a while until the soreness is either reduced or disappears entirely. Prolonged and progressive soreness is usually an indication of an overworked muscle. If you continue in your workouts, ignoring the warning sign, your chances of sustaining an injury become much greater.

---

In weight training, you can _____ the intensity of your workout.

CONTROL

If your muscles are still a little tight after warming up and stretching out, it is a good idea to _____ the intensity of your workout for that day.

REDUCE

If your muscles grow progressively sorer week after week, it is an indication that you are _____ and should decrease the intensity of your workout for a while.

OVERTRAINING

Ignoring muscle soreness and not reducing the intensity of your workout is inviting potential _____ .

INJURY

---

## STRETCHING EXERCISES

For those who enjoy stretching before lifting, the exercises indicated in Figures 13.2 through 13.11 will be much more effective after you have warmed up. If stretching makes you feel good and prepares you mentally for your workout, then, by all means stretch. For those of you who are not inclined to stretch, as long as you warm-up properly, your chances of injury are no greater than those of the person who has taken time to stretch.

**Figure 13.2.** *SHOULDERS: Join hands behind your back and interlock your fingers. Raise your arms as high as possible behind your back while keeping your elbows straight.*

**Figure 13.3.** *BACK (LATS): Join hands above your head and interlock your fingers. Keeping your elbows straight, try to reach, or stretch, your arms as high as possible over your head.*

**Figure 13.4.** *BACK OF ARM (TRICEPS): Bend one arm at the elbow and place it above and behind your head. Taking your other arm, reach across and behind your head and grab the opposite arm at the elbow. Pull that arm back slowly until you feel a mild stretch.*

**Figure 13.5.** *SIDES (OBLIQUES): Place one arm above your head and bend at the waist toward the opposite side. Try to keep your arm straight since it will accentuate the stretching on that side.*

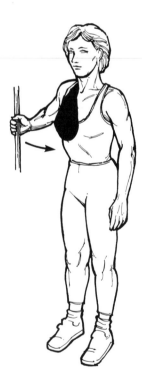

**Figure 13.6.** *CHEST (PECTORALS): Keeping one arm straight and off to the side, find something to hold that will prevent your arm from coming forward when you try to move it. The further your arm is out to your side and behind you, the greater the stretch on the chest.*

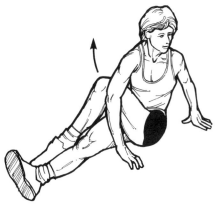

**Figure 13.7.** *OUTSIDE OF HIP (ABDUCTORS): Cross one leg over the other and place your opposite arm on the outside of the leg that is bent and doing the crossing. Press against the knee with your arm until you feel a stretch on the outside of your hip.*

**Figure 13.8.** *LOWER BACK/HAMSTRINGS: Sitting on the floor with your legs straight, reach forward until you feel a mild stretch on the back of your thighs. A variation of this stretch can be done with your legs apart.*

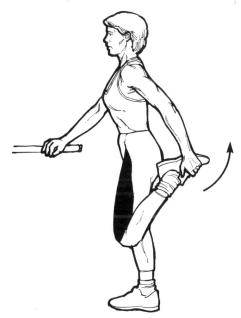

**Figure 13.9.** *FRONT THIGH (QUADRICEPS): Holding onto something with one arm for balance, grab the opposite foot and pull it up behind you. Gradually pull up and back on the foot until you feel a mild stretch on the front part of the thigh.*

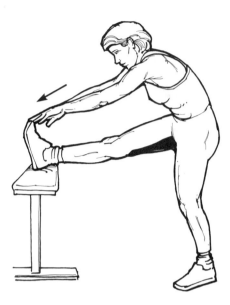

**Figure 13.10.** *BACK THIGH (HAMSTRINGS): Place one leg on a table or something that can support it about waist high. Keeping the leg as straight as possible, reach forward with both arms until you feel a mild stretch on the back part of your thigh.*

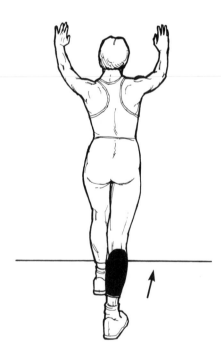

**Figure 13.11.** *CALF (GASTROC): With one foot in front of the other and both hands on a wall, lean into the wall, keeping the heel of your back foot straight and on the floor. Lean forward until you feel a stretch in the mid-portion of your calf.*

# 14

# Conditioning the Stomach

Although most people know relatively little about various aspects of fitness, they are familiar with the sit-up and its impact on the stomach, or abdominal, muscle. Unfortunately, there is a lot of misinformation concerning the proper way to do this exercise. When performed incorrectly, sit-ups can actually weaken rather than strengthen the stomach. In addition, they can tighten already strong hip flexor muscles, resulting in an excessive curve (lordosis) in the lower back (Figure 14.1).

## TRIMMING THE WAISTLINE—DIET, EXERCISE, AND SIT-UPS

Many males mistakenly believe that sit-ups can rectify or retard the bulging waistline that is characteristic of the "middle-age spread" (women deposit fat mainly around their hips and thighs). The expansion of the abdomen, however, represents an excess of adipose tissue (fat), not necessarily soft, flabby muscles. Although sit-ups will help strengthen and tighten the stomach muscles, they will neither help define nor reduce the waistline. The adipose tissue that lies between the abdomen and the skin will still make the stomach look soft and the waistline expanded no matter how many sit-ups are done. Only aerobic exercise (running, bicycling, aerobic dance, etc.) and dieting will, in effect, reduce adipose tissue in the body and, subsequently, the waistline. Therefore, trimming the waistline involves a three-pronged approach: aerobic activity, dieting, and sit-ups. Sit-ups, by themselves, will have little impact on the stomach if the individual does nothing else to reduce body fat.

### The Myth of Spot Reducing

It is a mistaken belief that you can reduce fat from specific areas in your body. Whenever you burn more calories than you take in, fat will be released from deposits located throughout the body to make up the difference. The fact that you are doing sit-ups doesn't mean that your body will use the fat from the stomach area. Unfortunately, exercising certain muscles has little to do with the release of fat from specific storage deposits in the body.

### Childbirth

Women particularly can benefit from sit-ups after childbirth. The longer the stomach muscles remain in a stretched state after childbirth, the harder it becomes for them to return to their previous condition. Subsequent births will further stretch the weakened muscles, adding to the pouched stomach appearance that many women have after bearing children. This condition can be minimized or prevented by diligent exercising of the

Normal

Anterior Pelvic Tilt

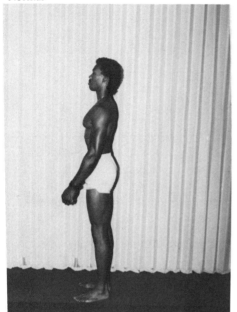

**Figure 14.1.** *Posture showing anterior tilting of the pelvis with accompanying excessive curvature in the lower back (lordosis).*

stomach muscles after childbirth. In this particular situation, the softness in the stomach area is caused by stretched and weakened abdominal muscles, not excess fat.

---

Doing sit-ups incorrectly can actually _____ (STRENGTHEN, WEAKEN) the abdominal muscles.

WEAKEN

If you further strengthen the already strong hip flexor muscle group by doing sit-ups improperly, it could pull the pelvis forward and accentuate the curve in the _____ _____ region.

LOWER BACK

Doing sit-ups (WILL, WILL NOT) reduce the waistline.

WILL NOT

The main factor that makes the stomach look soft is _____ lying between the muscle and skin, not necessarily soft, flabby muscles.

FAT

A three-pronged approach of _____ , _____ , and _____ is necessary to reduce the waistline.

DIET, AEROBIC EXERCISE, SIT-UPS

There _____ (IS, IS NOT) any such thing as spot reducing (reducing fat in a specific area).

IS NOT

When there is a calorie deficit, the body will take the energy from fat deposits located _____ the body.

THROUGHOUT

---

## The Rectus Abdominis

As you can see from Figure 14.2, the major muscle in the stomach is called the rectus abdominis and is often referred to as "the abdominals." It extends from the sternum, or breast bone, to the pubic bones of the pelvis. The fibers of the muscle lie vertically, which means that, when they slide past each other, the stomach will contract vertically. This will result in the muscle exerting a pull on the sternum and the pelvis.

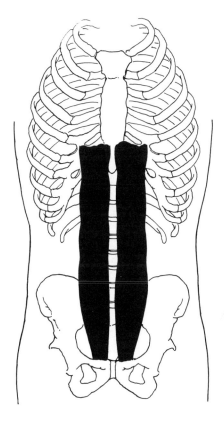

**Figure 14.2.** *The major muscle group of the abdomen, the rectus abdominis. Notice that it stretches from the sternum and upper rib cage to the pelvis.*

## PROPER ROM FOR A SIT-UP

When the pelvis is stabilized, the pull of the stomach muscles on the sternum is referred to as "trunk flexion." As you can see from Figure 14.3, trunk flexion only involves movement of the upper third of the back toward the hips. When the stomach contracts, it can only move the trunk this far. Any movement past this point will involve the hip flexors (Figure 14.4). Since the hip flexors are a deep muscle (they lie beneath the muscles of the thigh), they cannot be seen. Strengthening and developing them will do little for the physique and could cause problems with postural alignment of the pelvis.

As you can see from Figure 14.4, a full sit-up not only strengthens the abdominal muscles but the hip flexor muscles as well. Since this is not a particularly desirable result, any sit-up or variation should primarily involve a very small range of motion (ROM) and eliminate as much as possible any hip flexor movements. Also, once the individual has

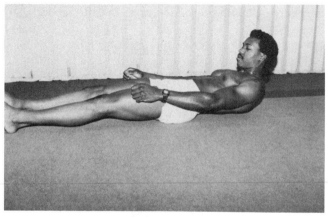

**Figure 14.3.** *When the rectus abdominis contracts with the pelvis stabilized, it results in trunk flexion. Notice that the stomach is responsible for only lifting the upper part of the chest cavity off the floor.*

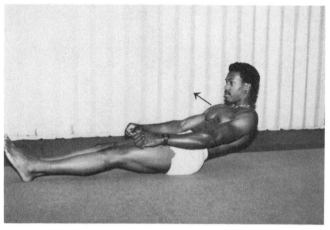

**Figure 14.4.** *Any movement past trunk flexion will result in hip flexor involvement. This picture illustrates the contribution of the hip flexors to the full sit-up.*

gone past a 45-degree angle in the ROM (Figure 14.5), due to body position and gravity, there is very little tension generated in the stomach muscles. This is further justification to eliminate much of the ROM in the traditional sit-up. An effective ROM for the sit-up is reflected in Figure 14.6.

**Figure 14.5.** *Since tension is being reduced in the stomach muscle from this point forward in the ROM, there is very little benefit in continuing.*

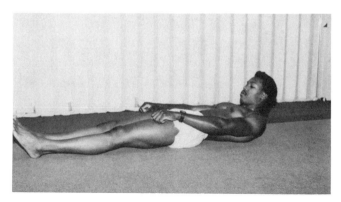

**Figure 14.6.** *An example of a good ROM for working the abdomen. Notice that all those parts of the ROM of a full sit-up that contribute little to strengthening the stomach have been eliminated.*

### Hooking the Feet

Many people question whether they should hook their feet to something when doing a sit-up. It has been my observation that, once the stomach muscle starts to get fatigued, people will use their legs to complete the repetitions if their feet are attached to something. With your feet unattached, it is very difficult to use anything but your stomach and hip flexors to perform the sit-up.

With your feet attached, it is possible to do a sit-up without using your stomach muscles. When the back is arched (Figure 14.7), the lower back and hip flexor muscles are actually doing most of the work. The stomach is in a stretched position, which can lead to a weaker rather than stronger muscle. With your feet unattached, it is extremely difficult to assume this arched back position.

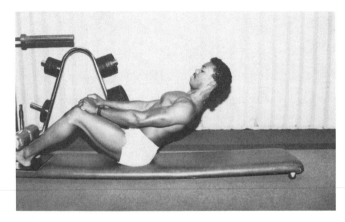

**Figure 14.7.** *An example of an incorrect way to perform a sit-up. Whenever you assume an arched-back position when doing a sit-up, it is possible to actually weaken the stomach muscles rather than strengthen them.*

## CORRECT POSITION OF THE SPINE

When strengthening the abdomen, always try to maintain a "C" *curve* position of the spine (Figure 14.8). Placing your arms out in front of you encourages this position of the back when performing the sit-up (Figure 14.9). Placing your hands behind your head has a tendency to encourage a straight, or arched, back position, which should be avoided.

## LEG POSITION

When doing a sit-up, it really does not matter whether your legs are bent or straight. The reason for bending the knees has been that it put the hip flexor muscles on slack so they could not contribute as much in performing the sit-up. However, any movement past trunk flexion (Figure 14.4), regardless of leg position, has to involve the hip flexors. It is far more important to concentrate on creating tension in the stomach than worry about the positioning of your legs.

**Figure 14.8.** *The correct "C" curve position of the spine when doing a sit-up. Whenever you work the stomach, you want your back to be curved.*

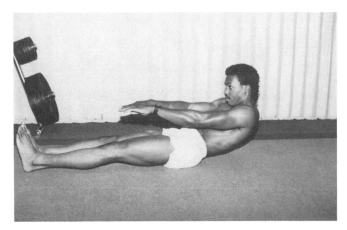

**Figure 14.9.** *Doing a sit-up with your arms out in front. This position encourages a curved spine. Placing your hands behind your head can lead to an arched-back position.*

## Too Many Repetitions

If you get to the point of being able to do hundreds of sit-ups in one set, you are probably getting very little benefit from the majority of them. You may be doing them so fast that momentum is doing most of the work rather than your stomach. Or, perhaps, you have become so efficient at the movement that the stomach muscle doesn't have to work as hard. Either way, I would suggest changing your routine and doing a different, perhaps more difficult, variation of the sit-up to place a stress on the stomach much earlier in the set. Whenever it takes hundreds of repetitions to get an adequate stress on any muscle, you should try to find another, more intense, way to work the muscle so that you don't have to do as many repetitions.

The stomach muscle is responsible for _____ (FLEXING, EXTENDING) the trunk.

FLEXING

In doing a full sit-up, any movement past trunk flexion will involve what muscle group?

HIP FLEXORS

The hip flexors are a deep muscle group, which means that they _____ (DO, DO NOT) lie next to the surface of the skin.

DO NOT

A good reason for eliminating a large part of the range of motion of a sit-up is that, after you get past a certain point (45-degree angle), most of the _____ is reduced in the stomach muscle.

TENSION

When working the stomach muscle, the spine should be in a _____ ("C" CURVE, ARCHED) position.

"C" CURVE

Whenever you arch your back when working your stomach, you are actually stretching it and, thus, _____ it.

WEAKENING

With your feet unattached, you _____ (CAN, CANNOT) use your legs to assist in doing the sit-up movement.

CANNOT

With your feet attached to something, it _____ (IS, IS NOT) possible to do a sit-up using your hip flexors and lower back and hardly work your stomach muscle at all.

IS

It _____ (IS, IS NOT) necessary to bend your knees when doing the sit-up.

IS NOT

If you are able to do hundreds of sit-ups before feeling any stress on your stomach, it is a good sign that you should _____ your routine so you will feel something much sooner in your workout.

REARRANGE OR CHANGE

# STOMACH EXERCISES

This section introduces a variety of acceptable exercises for strengthening the abdomen (Figures 14.10 to 14.20). All of these exercises can be incorporated into some type of circuit so you don't have to repeat any set more than one time. The exercises from Figures 14.15 through 14.17 are more advanced and should only be attempted after you have mastered the exercises preceding them (Figures 14.10 to 14.14). If you cannot maintain a "C" curve position of the spine with these variations, you should not continue to do them. The exercises from Figures 14.18 through 14.20 place a little more stress on the lower part of the abdominals.

**Figure 14.10.** *HANDS TO KNEES: From the starting sit-up position, chin on chest and shoulders off the mat (trunk flexion), roll forward until your hands come to the top of your knees. Hold that position for one second and repeat, working up to 40 repetitions.*

**Figure 14.11.** *HANDS CLASPED: From the starting sit-up position with your hands clasped together in front of you and your legs spread apart, roll forward until your lower back is off the mat. Hold that position for one second and repeat, working up to 40 repetitions.*

**Figure 14.12.** *CRUNCHES: With your knees bent and your hands behind your head, roll forward until your elbows touch your knees. Hold that position for one second and repeat, working up to 40 repetitions. A more difficult variation of this sit-up would consist of touching your elbows to your knees, two, three, or more times before returning to the starting position.*

**Figure 14.13.** BICYCLES: While doing a bicycling motion with your legs, touch one knee with your opposite elbow and repeat. Work up to 40 complete repetitions.

**Figure 14.14.** TOE TOUCHES: With your legs straight up in the air (knees can be slightly bent), reach as high as you can in an attempt to touch your toes. Hold that for one second and repeat, working up to 40 repetitions.

**Figure 14.15.** *ARM RAISES: With your back off the mat and your torso at a 45 degree angle, raise your arms up toward your head, keeping your elbows straight. Repeat this arm action three to six times before returning to the starting position. Repeat five to 10 times.*

**Figure 14.16.** *FLYAWAYS: With the same starting position as Figure 14.15, move your arms out to your sides with your elbows bent. Repeat this arm action three to six times before returning to the starting position. Repeat five to 10 times. Note: The farther out you move your arms in an arcing motion, the greater the stress placed on the stomach.*

**Figure 14.17.** *TWISTS: With the same starting position as Figure 14.15, hold your hands together and twist from side to side. Repeat the twists three to six times before returning to the starting position. Repeat five to 10 times. Note: The more you twist, the greater the stress placed on the stomach.*

**Figure 14.18.** *LEG BICYCLES: With your upper body supported by your elbows, alternate bringing your legs to your chest. Repeat anywhere from 50 to 100 times.*

**Figure 14.19.** *LEG TUCKS: Sitting on a bench with your legs extended, bring both knees to your chest before returning to the starting position. Repeat 20 to 40 times.*

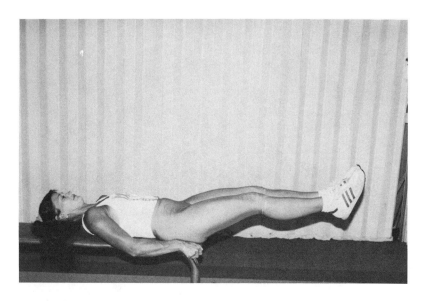

**Figure 14.20.** *LEG RAISES: Lying on a bench with your legs extended, raise them to a 90 degree position (knees can be slightly bent) before returning to the starting position. Repeat 20 to 40 times.*

# 15

# Understanding Injuries

Whenever you sustain an injury, there are two issues that need to be addressed in the rehabilitation process. The first is getting strength back to the injured part, and the second is regaining normal range of motion (flexibility). If one or both of these areas of concern are not given sufficient attention during the rehabilitation process, there could be a possibility of some chronic problems occurring with the injury.

## IMMOBILIZATION AND ATROPHY

Two things happen to a muscle when you immobilize it for any period of time. The first and most obvious is that the muscle noticeably shrinks in size. This is called "atrophy," which is the *wasting away* of muscle tissue. Atrophy always occurs when a muscle remains inactive for any period of time. The degree of atrophy and loss of strength depends upon the length of inactivity.

## IMMOBILIZATION AND CONTRACTURE

The second thing that happens to an immobilized muscle is the *sticking together* of the protein filaments and connective tissue surrounding the individual muscle fibers. The result is a muscle that resists being stretched, thus limiting the flexibility around that particular joint. This phenomenon is referred to as "contracture" (not contraction) and will occur to some extent whenever a limb is immobilized. The longer the period of immobilization, the more firmly the contracture in the muscle. If the individual does not work on regaining flexibility in the joint, the range of motion loss could be permanent. Active stretching of the tightened muscle and the application of warm, moist heat are two good aids in regaining flexibility in the contractured muscle.

Although it may seem obvious that weight training is an excellent way to rehabilitate an injured muscle, it may not be quite so apparent why you should use weight training for rehabilitating an injured joint (ankle, knee, etc.). As you can see from Figure 15.1, a joint such as the knee is simply the axis or articulation of two bones. In this case, it is the femur (thigh bone) and tibia (shin bone). The knee joint derives its stability and strength from the ligaments and tendons that cross over it. Ligaments are a tough, somewhat flexible type of tissue that connect bone to bone. As you can see in Figure 15.1, the ligaments are so arranged that they provide stability to the knee joint. Tendons, on the other hand, connect muscle to bone. Since the tendons of muscles cross over joints, they, too, provide stability and strength to the joint. By strengthening the muscles above the

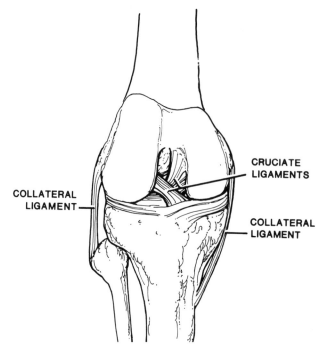

CRUCIATE
LIGAMENTS

COLLATERAL
LIGAMENT

COLLATERAL
LIGAMENT

**Figure 15.1.** *Illustration showing how ligaments provide stability to the knee joint.*

injured joint (thigh muscles for the knee, calf muscles for the ankle), you also strengthen both the tendons associated with those muscles and the ligaments of that particular joint. Consequently, the joint is strengthened and becomes more stable because of the weight training program. That is why some type of resistive exercise (usually weight training) is recommended in the rehabilitative process of an injured limb.

---

In rehabilitating an injured muscle, you have to consider two factors, _____ and _____ .

STRENGTH, FLEXIBILITY

Whenever a limb is immobilized, there will be a certain amount of _____ of muscle tissue.

LOSS OR ATROPHY

Whenever a limb is immobilized, there is also a certain amount of _____ that will occur.

CONTRACTURE

_____ is the sticking together of the fibers within a muscle.

CONTRACTURE

The longer a limb is immobilized, the _____ (GREATER, LESSER) the degree of atrophy and contracture.

GREATER

The longer you wait to rehabilitate a muscle after immobilization, the _____ (MORE LIKELY, LESS LIKELY) it is that the injury will never fully recover.

MORE LIKELY

Weight training _____ (DOES, DOES NOT) strengthen the ligaments and tendons surrounding a joint.

DOES

---

## SUPERIORITY OF ACCOMMODATING RESISTANCE

Accommodating resistance is clearly a superior type of resistance to use in rehabilitating an injured muscle. As you can see in Figure 15.2, a hypothetical example is given of the strength potential of a post-surgical knee joint. Although the strength potential indicated at each joint angle may not be realistic, the diagram illustrates one of the major advantages of using accommodating resistance in rehabilitating an injured limb. In this particular example, the individual would be forced to do knee extensions with two pounds using fixed or variable resistances since that represents the weakest point in the ROM. Obviously, other points in the ROM that could be strengthened more closely to the maximum potential are not because of the condition of the knee after surgery. With accommodating resistance, all points in the ROM receive a maximal stimulus regardless of their strength potential.

### Less Chance of Re-injury

Another problem with fixed or variable resistances involves the selection of a resistance that could end up straining the knee during the latter parts of the ROM. As you can see from Figure 15.2, even three pounds would result in overexertion of the knee at the end of the ROM. Consequently, it would be much easier to re-injure the knee using fixed or variable resistances. With accommodating resistance, however, you don't have the problem of selecting a resistance that is too much for the muscle to overcome (Figure 15.3). Since the machine matches only the force exerted by the lifter at all points in the ROM, the potential for overexerting and injuring the knee is greatly reduced.

### Less Muscle Soreness

Another advantage of using accommodating resistance for rehabilitation is that it eliminates the eccentric phase of a muscle contraction. If you recall from Chapter 7, the eccentric phase of a muscle contraction involves the lengthening of the muscles while it is still creating tension. Research has demonstrated quite conclusively that it is the eccentric phase, as opposed to the concentric or muscle-shortening phase, that results in greater muscle soreness. Thus, by eliminating the eccentric part of the muscle contraction, you minimize the amount of soreness that may occur in the injured limb. This would, obviously, tend to speed up the recovery process and further reduce the chances of re-injury.

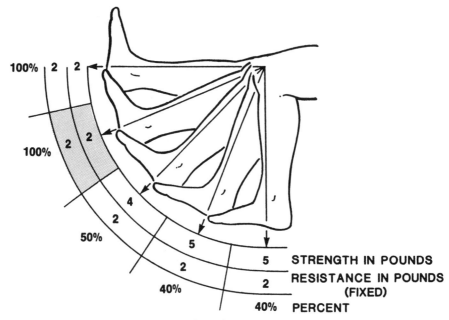

**Figure 15.2.** *Hypothetical vector diagram of the strength of a knee joint after surgery. With fixed or variable resistances, the individual could only use two pounds of resistance (weakest point in ROM).*

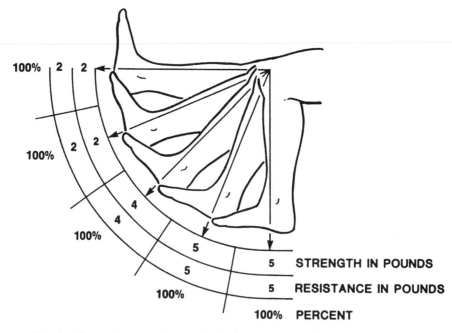

**Figure 15.3.** *Hypothetical vector diagram of the strength of the knee joint showing all points in the ROM receiving maximal resistance with accommodating resistance.*

Taking all of these factors into consideration, less chance of re-injury, less muscle soreness and greater development of strength through the ROM, there is absolutely no question that accommodating resistance is superior to either fixed or variable resistance for rehabilitating an injured muscle or limb. Most sports medicine physicians today use accommodating resistance machines in their clinics for rehabilitative purposes.

---

Which type of resistance (FIXED, VARIABLE, ACCOMMODATING) is clearly superior for rehabilitation of an injured muscle?

ACCOMMODATING

It _____ (IS POSSIBLE, IS NOT POSSIBLE) to strain an injured muscle further with fixed or variable resistances.

IS POSSIBLE

The _____ point of an injured limb is so low that with fixed or variable resistances you actually strengthen little else in the range of motion.

WEAKEST

With _____ resistance, the machine matches the force exerted by the lifter.

ACCOMMODATING

Which phase of the muscle contraction results in more muscle soreness, the concentric (muscle shortening) or eccentric (muscle lengthening)?

ECCENTRIC

With accommodating resistance, there is _____ (LESS, MORE) muscle soreness.

LESS

Which type of resistance involves only the concentric phase of a muscle contraction (FIXED, VARIABLE, ACCOMMODATING)?

ACCOMMODATING

Which type of resistance results in greater strength development throughout the entire range of motion (FIXED, VARIABLE, ACCOMMODATING)?

ACCOMMODATING

---

## Pain of Muscle Injury

First of all, it is important to know the different types of pain you may experience in a weight room and how much concern you should give each one. Whenever you lift and experience a *sudden, sharp, intense pain*, quit immediately. Do not try to do more repetitions or work through the pain. This type of pain should be a signal that you are doing damage to your muscles. If, after a brief rest period, you attempt to do another set and the pain reappears, it is further confirmation that you have injured yourself.

## Pain of Fatigue

The pain of muscle fatigue is much different. If you feel a *gradual burning sensation* in your muscles as the result of doing numerous repetitions, this is normal and you need not worry about the possibility of injuring yourself. Usually, the pain or burning sensation will intensify with each succeeding repetition until you are forced to stop to allow your muscles time to recover. After resting a short period (30-60 seconds), the pain should subside. Within a couple of minutes, you should be able to start another set or exercise without pain.

This type of burning pain is caused by the *accumulation* of *lactic acid* in the muscle, not tissue damage. The more repetitions that are completed as the muscle fatigues, the greater the accumulation of lactic acid. Many athletes actually don't feel like they are getting an adequate workout until they experience this burning sensation in their muscles.

Thus, the pain of muscle fatigue is much different than the pain of injury. Any sharp pain that comes on suddenly and occurs anytime during the set is a pain of muscle injury, and you should stop immediately.

## WORKING AROUND MUSCLE SORENESS

The injuries incurred in weight training are usually not debilitating. They develop from soreness in the muscle that grows progressively worse with training. Eventually, the soreness develops into a slight pull or tear of part of the muscle that elicits pain with some movements. Before quitting your workouts altogether, however, there are some alternatives you should try to keep your training going.

First, try doing the same exercise(s) that are giving you pain but with lighter weight. If that doesn't seem to alleviate the problem, try changing grips from narrow to wide, or vice versa, and see if that has any effect on reducing the pain. For example, changing to a narrow grip seems to be effective in reducing anterior deltoid (shoulder) pain when doing the bench press (Figure 15.4). Often, changing from free bars and machines to dumbbells can also help. As you can see from Figure 15.5, by keeping the palms facing in, the lifter is able to do a bicep curl without straining the tendons that cross over the inside of the elbow joint. If none of these techniques work, try doing another exercise that works the same muscle group. For example, instead of using the bench press to work the chest, you can substitute "flys" or push-ups. It is possible that you may be able to exercise a muscle another way without pain.

Thus, your first response to muscle soreness should be to try working around the soreness without aggravating it further. If you have to eliminate working a muscle group (say biceps) but can do the rest of your routine, by all means do so. Don't let the soreness in one muscle group prevent you from working out completely. However, if you have tried all of the above techniques and you still have pain lifting, then it is probably in your best interest to refrain from working out until you can do so without pain.

**Figure 15.4.** *By changing the grip in the bench press from wide (a) to narrow (b), it often is helpful in alleviating pain in the front part of the shoulder (anterior deltoid).*

## TREATING AN INJURY

Whenever you injure yourself, always apply ice for the first 24 to 48 hours and then heat after that time period. Many people mistakenly apply heat during that time, which can actually accentuate tissue swelling and prolong the recovery period. Also, whenever you aggravate an old injury, apply ice to reduce the inflammation. If you are in doubt concerning which treatment to apply, ice is always the safest choice. Applying heat too early to an injury can cause problems.

Once you are able to apply heat to your injury, warm, moist, circulating heat (hot whirlpool) is the most effective. Topical lotions applied to the skin do not penetrate to the muscle, consequently, they promote little healing. Deep heat will encourage healing by bringing oxygen and nutrients to the damaged tissue.

**Figure 15.5.** *By using dumbbells when performing the bicep curl, you don't have to rotate the wrist, which may help in alleviating pain in the inside of the elbow.*

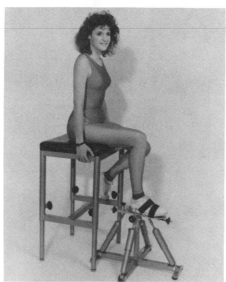

**Figure 15a.** *A machine designed to strengthen the ankle and shin. Since it allows rotary as well as back and forth movements, it is very effective for rehabilitating an injured ankle. Courtesy of Wikco Industries, Inc., Broken Bow, NE.*

Whenever you experience a sharp, intense pain in your workout, you should _____ immediately.

STOP OR QUIT

A gradual burning sensation in your muscles with continued repetitions is a pain of _____ (FATIGUE, INJURY).

FATIGUE

Pain caused by fatigue _____ (WILL, WILL NOT) subside within a couple of minutes.

WILL

Pain caused by muscle injury _____ (WILL, WILL NOT) subside within a couple of minutes.

WILL NOT

The pain of muscle fatigue is caused by the accummulation of _____ _____ in the muscle and surrounding tissue.

LACTIC ACID

If you have muscle soreness, one option is to use _____ (LIGHTER, HEAVIER) weight.

LIGHTER

Another option for working a muscle group that is tight or sore is to _____ your grip.

CHANGE

A third option is to try a _____ exercise that works the same muscle group.

DIFFERENT

If all three options above fail, then it is best to perhaps _____ working that particular muscle group until the soreness goes away.

STOP

Progressive muscle soreness from weight training is a good indication that you should _____ the intensity of your workouts.

BACK OFF OR REDUCE

You should always apply _____ (ICE, HEAT) to an injury during the first 24 to 48 hours.

ICE

Whenever you irritate an existing injury, you should always apply _____ (ICE, HEAT) in treating it.

ICE

Applying heat too soon to an injury will only tend to cause more _____ in the tissue.

SWELLING/INFLAMMATION

The most penetrating type of heat to the muscles is _____ (MOIST, TOPICAL LOTIONS).

MOIST

# 16

# Safety in the Weight Room

Although weight training is a relatively safe sport, there are certain circumstances that are potentially dangerous if lifters have not been properly instructed. As with most accidents, common sense and concentration can help prevent them. Most injuries occur because individuals have extended themselves beyond their capabilities or they have failed to follow some simple safety guidelines. Hopefully, the information presented in this chapter will help you become aware of some of the safety concerns in the weight room as well as avoid the possibility of injuring yourself.

## CARE OF THE BACK

One of the areas that you have to be concerned about in weight training is the back. If you overextend yourself, some of the exercises designed to strengthen this area also have the potential to injure it. There are basically two movements involving the back that can place it in jeopardy. The first movement involves bending at the waist and primarily results in the back muscles being overstretched, while the second movement involves excessive arching of the back and results in compression of the discs that lie between the vertebrae of the spine.

The group of muscles that support and move the back are referred to as the *erector spinae* (Figure 16.1). Notice that they run longitudinally along the spinal column. When they contract, they are responsible for extension of the trunk (Figure 16.2). Bending at the waist, which is the opposite action of trunk extensions, stretches these muscles.

The exercises in Figure 16.3 indicate potential ways in which you could overstretch the back muscles. Notice that all of them involve bending motions while supporting some type of resistance. These exercises are designed to strengthen the back. However, they can easily strain it if the resistance is too great. Consequently, you need to be aware of the potential problem with these exercises. Figure 16.4 shows a much safer exercise that works the back. Notice that in this exercise, you are basically doing an isometric contraction (tension without movement), which strengthens the back while eliminating the possibility of overstretching the muscles.

The other way to injure the back involves herniation, or rupture of the discs between the vertebrae from compression of the spinal column. This could be due to either excessive arching or bending of the back. Figure 16.5 shows some exercises that have the potential to put an excessive strain on the spinal column. Notice that all of these exercises involve arching the back while there is compression on the spinal column. Performing these exercises with a straight or flat back somewhat reduces the potential for injuring the discs.

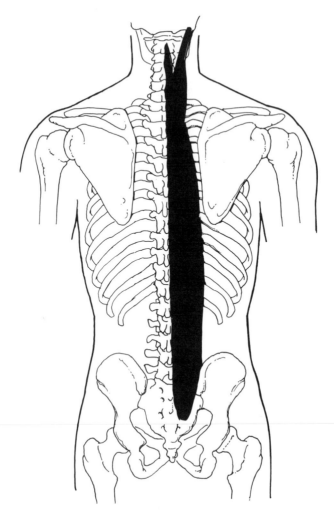

**Figure 16.1.** *The erector spinae, the major muscle group supporting the lower back.*

If you have ever had back problems, consider using a weight belt (Figure 16.6) for extra support. The belt does take some pressure off the lower back, particularly with exercises involving an arched-back position. It provides less support in bending exercises that stretch the back muscles.

## Stretch, Not Strengthen, the Back

Contrary to what most people think, they do not need to strengthen the back as much as they need to stretch it out and make it more flexible. More back injuries are caused by overstretching (bending) than by muscle weakness. A flexible back would help minimize the chance of a muscle pull when it is stretched. Consequently, it is important to

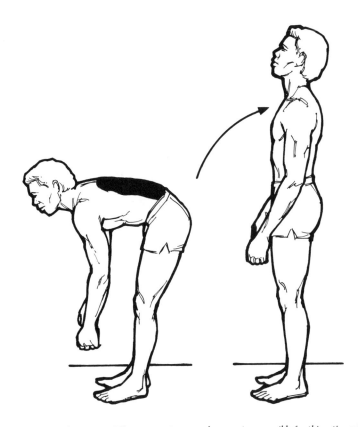

**Figure 16.2.** *The movement of trunk extension. The erector spinae muscle group is responsible for this action when it contracts.*

**Figure 16.3.** *Exercises that could potentially overstretch the erector spinae muscle group and cause lower back injury. It is important to use caution when performing these movements.*

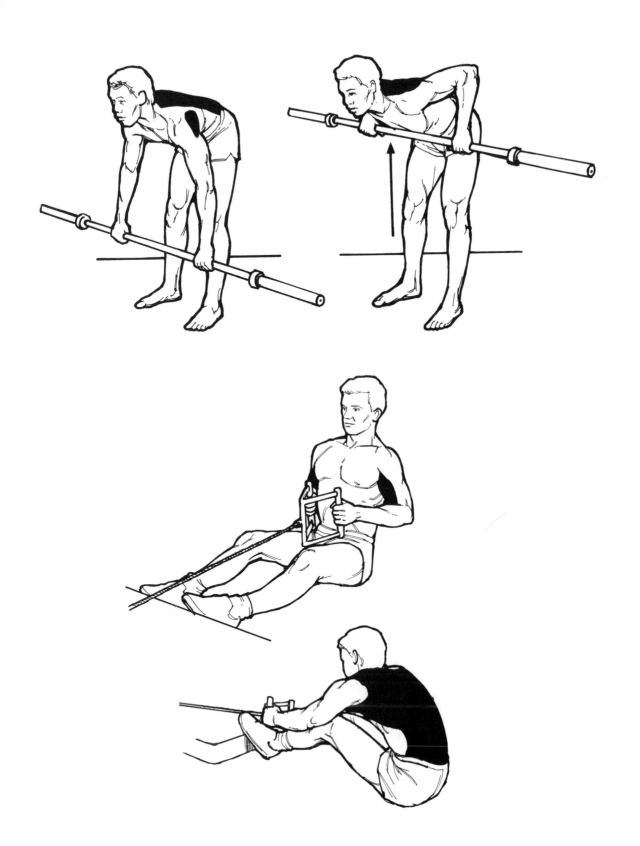

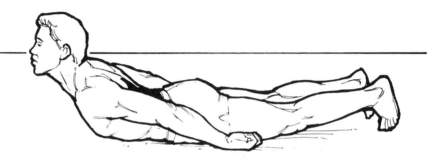

**Figure 16.4.** *A much safer way to strengthen the lower back muscles without risking the possibility of overstretching them. Notice that the movement of trunk flexion (bending at the waist) is completely eliminated.*

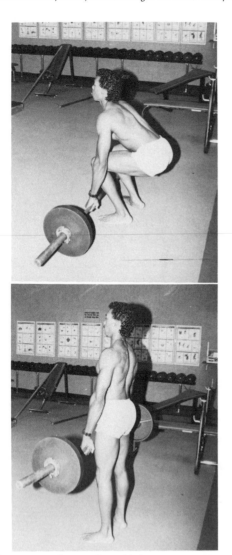

**Figure 16.5.** *Exercises that could place excessive pressure on the discs in the lower back, causing injury. Notice all of these exercises involve compression with excessive arching in the lower back region. a. Dead Lift, b. Bent-Over Flys, c. Bench Press, d. Shoulder Press, e. Squat, f. Back Hyperextensions, g. Hamstring Curl.*

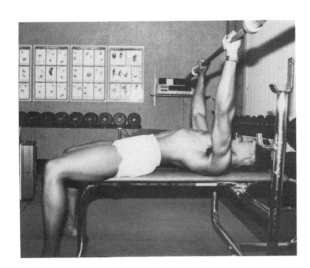

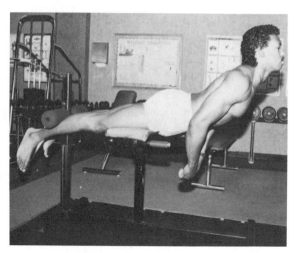

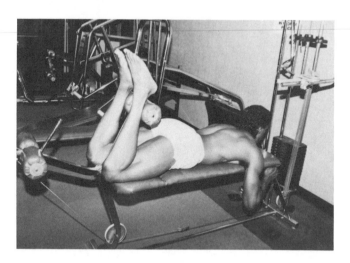

**Figure 16.6.** *A weight belt can help take pressure off the lower back, especially when performing exercises involving arching of the back. Most decent belts cost from $20 to $30.*

incorporate some stretching exercises for the back in your program. This becomes exceedingly critical as you age. Figures 16.14 through 16.19 at the end of this chapter illustrate some exercises that stretch the back and spinal column with minimal risk of injury.

---

There are two potential ways of injuring the back in the weight room. The first is by _____ the muscles in the back by bending at the waist.

STRETCHING

The second is by _____ the vertebrae in the spinal column by excessive arching or bending.

COMPRESSING

The back muscles (erector spinae) are responsible for trunk _____ (FLEXION, EXTENSION).

EXTENSION

Bending at the waist _____ (STRETCHES, SHORTENS) the back muscles.

STRETCHES

A weight belt would help with what type of back problem in the weight room (OVERSTRETCHING, COMPRESSION)?

COMPRESSION

Most backs are _____ (STRONG, FLEXIBLE) enough but do need to develop more _____ (STRENGTH, FLEXIBILITY).

STRONG, FLEXIBILITY

---

## GRIPPING THE BAR

It is a good idea, as a beginning lifter, to get used to gripping any bar with your thumbs wrapped around it. Although this may seem elementary, many experienced lifters use what is called a "cheaters grip" (Figure 16.7) when doing bench, incline and shoulder presses. They use this grip because they feel it places their wrists in a more advantageous position for a firmer push. With this grip, however, there is absolutely no way that you could prevent the bar from slipping out of your hands. Although this may never occur with an experienced lifter, such an accident can result in serious injury or death. Wrappings your thumbs around the bar completely eliminates this possibility.

Whenever you grab a bar or handle on a machine, make sure that your grip is even from side to side. As you can see in Figure 16.8, if you lift with an uneven grip, it is possible to develop asymmetrically and to injure yourself since one side of your body is assuming a much greater portion of stress than the other side.

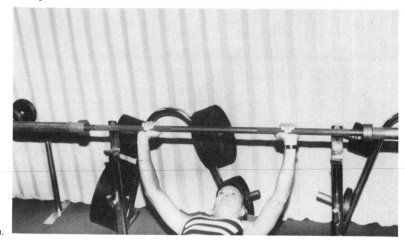

a.

b.

**Figure 16.7.** *a. "Cheaters grip" primarily used for the bench and shoulder presses. Notice that the thumbs are not placed around the bar. This grip is extremely dangerous since the lifter cannot prevent the bar from slipping out of her hands. b. Proper grip with thumbs wrapped around the bar.*

**Figure 16.8.** *Grabbing the bar with an uneven grip can result in asymmetrical muscle development as well as increasing the potential for injury. Always line up your grip from side to side to make sure that it is even.*

## USE OF MACHINES

There are several reasons for using machines rather than free weights (bars and dumbbells), but the most important one has to do with *safety*. With free weights, there is always the possibility that the bar can slip out of your hands and fall on you. With machines, this problem is completely eliminated. Machines also provide an advantage in allowing *particular movements* that cannot be duplicated with free weights. In addition, they are sometimes able to *isolate* a specific muscle more effectively than free weights and *enhance range* of *motion*. Beginners should start on machines, if available, then gradually work their way over to free weights. Since they don't have to worry about injuring themselves with machines, they can devote all of their attention to lifting and developing proper technique.

## SPOTTING THE BENCH PRESS

I advocate one person spotting for this lift rather than two simply because two people can never grab the bar at precisely the same moment. If one spotter grabs the bar slightly before the other spotter, all of the weight will shift to one side (Figure 16.9). This sudden, unexpected shifting of weight can cause an injury. With one person spotting in the middle (Figure 16.10), this problem is eliminated.

The spotter's responsibilities are to help raise the bar off the stand if the lifter so asks and, more important, to guide it back to the stand when the lifter has completed her set.

**Figure 16.9.** *The shifting of weight during the bench press because one spotter grabbed the bar before the other. This situation could lead to a serious muscle pull for the lifter since she was not expectng the sudden weight shift to that side of the body.*

**Figure 16.10.** *With one person spotting from the middle on the bench press, the problem of coordination between two spotters is eliminated.*

The spotter is also there to make sure the bar does not fall on the lifter as well as to assist the lifter in completing some of her last repetitions when fatigued.

## Bench Press Stands

It is important to realize that the width of the stands on the bench press can affect safety. With bench presses that have wide stands (Figure 16.11), it is possible to leave weights on one side and remove them from the other side without the bar tipping over. On the other hand, for bench presses with narrow stands (Figure 16.12), you have to be

**Figure 16.11.** *Wide bench press stand. This makes the bench much safer since weight can be taken off one side without having the bar tip over.*

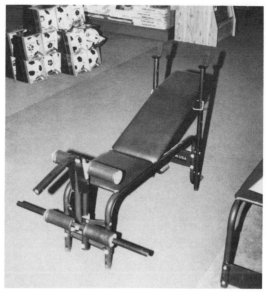

**Figure 16.12.** *Narrow incline press stand. You have to be extremely careful with this stand since taking weight off of one side could tip the bar over. Courtesy of Herman's World of Sporting Goods, Sunnyvale, CA.*

extremely careful since removing weight from one side may cause an imbalance of the bar so it tips over. Many benches marketed for home use have a narrow stand. Therefore, it is important to be cautious when putting on or taking off weights. Of course, the same precaution applies to incline or decline bench stands as well (Figure 16.13).

## BREATHING

Although if left to their natural instincts most people will breathe correctly when lifting weights, it is important to understand the right way to breath and the consequences of incorrect breathing. Whenever you contract muscle, your blood pressure rises dramatically. In addition, if you hold your breath, the pressure in the chest cavity increases, raising blood pressure still further (referred to as the Valsalva maneuver). It is possible to black out if the pressure builds too high. *Exhaling* while lifting will reduce pressure in the chest cavity, thus decreasing the possibility of this effect occurring. It is important, therefore, from a safety standpoint, to understand that you should *never hold your breath* when lifting and that you should know when to *inhale* and *exhale*.

Without getting too specific and complicated, the easiest way to describe how to breathe is to follow this simple guideline: *Breathe in* when *pulling in, breathe out* when *pushing out.* If you follow your natural instincts and don't force your breathing, you will find that you may already do this without thinking about it. It is almost impossible for you to do otherwise when performing these movements. If you do have to think about when to breathe, however, this guideline should make it a lot simpler.

### Avoiding Traffic Flow Patterns of the Room

Try to do your free-weight lifting away from the natural traffic flow patterns of the room. If you lift in an area where people have to get around you to reach equipment, you run the risk of collision and injury. Whenever the weight you are lifting is suddenly shifted to one side of your body, you risk muscle strain. Consequently, it is in your best interest to avoid such occurrences.

---

It is always a good rule to get used to gripping a bar with your _____ wrapped around it.

THUMBS

Whenever you grab a bar with an uneven grip, you run the risk of developing asymmetrically as well as possibly _____ yourself.

INJURING

It is better to have _____ (ONE, TWO) spotter(s) on the bench press.

ONE

Wide bench press stands are _____ (MORE LIKELY, LESS LIKELY) to cause the bar to tip over when lifting weights off one side.

LESS LIKELY

Holding your breath when lifting will dramatically _____ blood pressure.

INCREASE OR ELEVATE

Pressure in the chest cavity can get so high from lifting that you can actually _____ _____ .

BLACK OUT

When pulling in, you should breathe _____ (IN, OUT).

IN

When pushing out, you should breathe _____ (IN, OUT).

OUT

Try to avoid lifting near the natural _____ patterns of the weight room since you may be bumped by someone and injure yourself.

FLOW

---

**Figure 16.13.** *Power rack showing pin placement to protect the lifter when performing the squat. Power racks make a significant contribution to the safety features in a weight room.*

## EXERCISES THAT STRETCH THE BACK

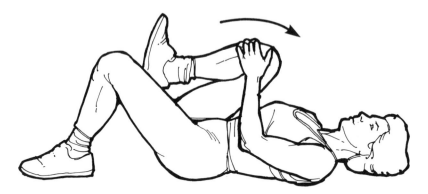

**Figure 16.13.** *Slowly bring your knee to your chest with both hands. Return to the starting position. Repeat, alternating legs five to 10 times.*

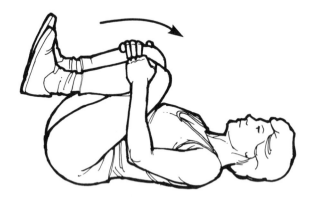

**Figure 16.14.** *Slowly bring your knees to your chest with your hands and hold for 20 to 30 seconds. Repeat five to 10 times.*

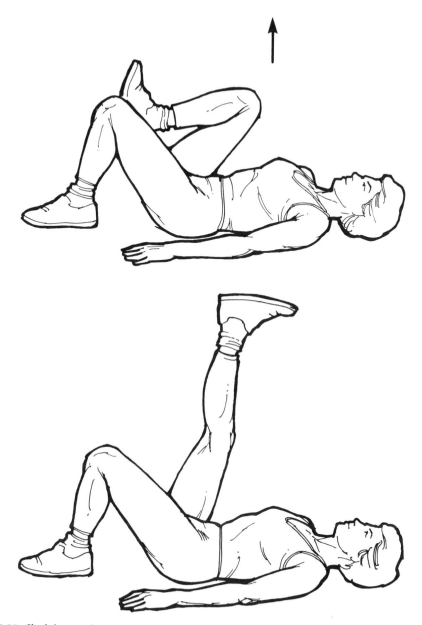

**Figure 16.15.** *Slowly bring one knee to your chest, then straighten it out as much as possible. Bend knee and return to starting position. Repeat, alternating legs five to 10 times.*

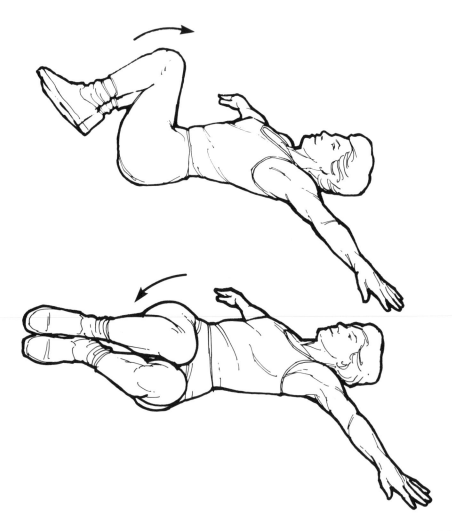

**Figure 16.16.** *Bend knees. While keeping them together, roll as far as you can from one side to the other. Keep your back flat on the floor. Repeat 10 times.*

**Figure 16.17.** *From your elbows, press the top half of your body upwards by extending, or straightening, your arms. Keep the lower half of your body in contact with the floor. Repeat 10 times.*

**Figure 16.18.** *With one leg extended and the other bent and crossed over it at the knee, press the knee to the opposite shoulder. Hold for five to 10 seconds and repeat 10 times for each leg.*

# 17

# Weight Training Through the Years

Although most of us would like to postpone the aging process, it is inevitable and will, in one way or another, impact our lives. The extent of that impact has a lot to do with the way you treat your body and how active and fit you are during the course of your lifetime. As you can see from Figure 17.1, what was once considered the normal aging process is now looked upon as more a function of disuse and inactivity (use it or lose it). Researchers are finding that people who stay active throughout their lives exhibit much less physical decline than the average individual. Therefore, you don't have to accept the stereotype that we normally attribute to the elderly. Although some of your physical capacities will decrease with age, if you keep active and exercise all of your life, you can maintain the strength, tone and definition that is normally associated with people much younger.

## AREAS AFFECTED BY AGING

For the purpose of this book, the specific areas of focus will include the skeletal system, the spinal column, muscle and body weight. As you will learn, training with weights can have a significant impact on all of these areas.

### The Skeletal System

It has been well-documented that certain minerals (calcium in particular) are lost from the skeletal system (bones) over the course of one's lifetime. This condition is called *osteoporosis* (thinning of bone). Minerals such as calcium give bone its strength and rigidity. A loss of minerals from bone will result in a weaker skeletal system that is more susceptible to fracturing. Women, after menopause, are much more prone to osteoporosis because of a decrease in the female hormone estrogen. However, with aging, both men and women are afflicted by this natural phenomenon to a certain extent.

Much of this mineral loss with aging can be attributed to poor nutrition (diet low in calcium) and lack of exercise. However, it has also been observed that periods of prolonged bed rest (three weeks or longer) can result in bone loss at any age. To a certain extent, then, the impact of osteoporosis can be minimized. Sound nutritional practices and exercise appear to be important components in maintaining a strong skeletal system.

Depending upon the forces and stresses applied to bones, structural changes can occur in the skeletal system. When less stress is applied, there is a greater efflux, or release, of calcium from the bones. With greater stress, more calcium is absorbed by the bones, which makes them stronger. Consequently, resistive exercise has the ability to minimize bone loss through one's life span. Those individuals who engage in a lifetime of

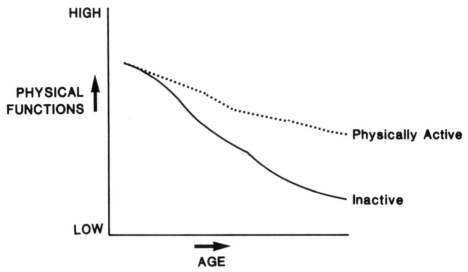

**Figure 17.1.** *Two theoretical curves showing loss of physical functions with age. People who are active all of their lives show much less physical degeneration than their inactive counterparts.*

regular exercise such as weight training tend to maintain much greater skeletal system integrity.

## Spinal Column

The spinal column is composed of bony structures called vertebrae that surround and protect the spinal cord from injury. Between the vetebrae lie cartilage-type discs that act as shock absorbers when the spinal column is compressed. It is these discs that can be pinched (herniated) or ruptured when the spinal column is compressed, causing serious back problems.

With aging, these discs lose their water content, becoming rigid and inelastic. This action results in a decrease in size of the spinal column and of the individual as well. As these discs lose their elastic and shock-absorption properties, the back becomes more inflexible and rigid. Consequently, movements of the spinal column that were done easily during youth can cause serious back strain in adulthood.

Much of the rigidity in the back that comes with aging can be attributed to a lack of activity and exercise of the spinal column. If the spinal column is actively exercised as one ages, it will be more likely to endure the compression stresses and forces that are placed upon it. Individuals who do no exercise at all are in real jeopardy of injuring their backs when they are confronted with placing an unaccustomed stress on their spinal columns. In that situation, the rigid cartilage discs are more likely to rupture than absorb the stress. Training with weights will help keep the discs flexible as well as provide support for the back by strengthening the ligaments and muscles surrounding the spinal column. Chapter 16 addresses more specifically some of the concerns in exercising the back.

**Figure 17.2.** *Helen Zechmeister performing a squat at age 82. Helen started powerlifting at the age of 76 and works out two hours every day. She has bench pressed 100 pounds and deadlifted 235 pounds. Helen has been written up in* Sports Illustrated *and appeared on David Letterman's show "Growing Up Is Not For Sissies."*

## Muscle

The average, non-active individual loses approximately 30 percent of his muscle tissue throughout his lifetime. Obviously, this loss of muscle tissue will significantly affect strength capacity. With fewer protein filaments in the muscle available to slide past each other, the ability of the muscle to generate force is significantly reduced.

The loss of muscle tissue is caused by a decrease in the number and size of the muscle cells or fibers (Chapter 10). In addition, since the size of the motor unit is reduced due to a reduction in muscle fibers, the individual has to activate more motor units to generate the same degree of force. This is perceived by the individual as an increase in effort, which makes it difficult to sustain through one's lifetime.

This decrease in strength starts to occur around the age of 35 for most people, but is not consistent for every muscle group in the body. Some muscle groups experience a greater reduction in strength than others. People who train with weights do not experience nearly as much reduction in muscle function with age. They are able to retain more protein filaments in their muscle fibers as well as maintain good neuromuscular activation. Thus, they are able to realize good muscle tone, size and definition as well as strength throughout their lifetime. Although they may not be able to lift as much as they did when they were younger, there is no comparison between these individuals and the average, sedentary adult. There is no reason to accept anything but firm, defined muscles throughout your life as long as you use them and keep them active.

## Body Weight

Although many people believe that putting on weight is part of the normal aging process, older individuals in primitive cultures show no such increase. The increase in body weight and body fat observed in the adult in Western cultures is the result of inactivity and poor nutritional habits (overeating). Unfortunately, metabolism slows down approximately 15 percent over the course of one's life span because the body does not need as many calories for growth purposes. Eating habits, however, do not change over that time period to reflect the decrease in calories needed by the body. In addition, activity levels often drop off, which further reduces the number of calories needed. Consequently, as you age, it is very easy to add body weight and body fat by maintaining your eating habits and decreasing your activity levels.

Interestingly, it is possible to maintain the same weight as you age but increase your body fat percentage. As discussed above, if you do not exercise, you will lose a certain amount of muscle tissue over your life span. But, by maintaining the same weight, what you actually do is replace the muscle tissue you are losing with fat. This increases your overall percentage of body fat. Consequently, you may not be holding your own as you age if you maintain your body weight but don't exercise. It is only through such activities as weight training and aerobic exercise that you can deter the loss of muscle tissue as you age and maintain your present percentage of body fat.

Muscle burns calories (metabolically active) at rest, which is another factor in support of maintaining good muscle tone throughout your lifetime. Fat does not burn calories in any state. Therefore, the more muscle tissue you have, the higher your metabolism. Maintaining good muscle tone all of your life will deter the increase in body fat that normally accompanies the aging of a sedentary individual.

## TRAINING PROGRAMS

Obviously, the intensity of effort must be reduced somewhat as one ages. The degree of adjustment, of course, depends upon many factors, such as genetics, prior activity level

**Figure 17.3.** *The masters (over 40) age group competitors at the Santa Cruz Muscle Beach contest show you don't have to accept a flabby, unconditioned body as you get older. The oldest competitor at 48 (second from the right) won the contest.*

and mental attitude. While one person may maintain excellent strength throughout his lifetime, someone else may lose strength rapidly. Those who are inactive will realize a greater reduction in overall strength than those who are active.

As you age, there should be a gradual reduction in the amount of weight used with a subsequent increase in the number of repetitions per set. You should de-emphasize a pure strength routine involving heavy weights and few repetitions. At this point in your life, the concern should be on maintaining strength already developed rather than on increasing it. Since your muscles and tendons have lost some of their suppleness and pliability with age, overexerting could result in a greater possibility of injury.

## Routine

Because much depends on the condition of the lifter, it is difficult to establish a specific routine. Performing 10 to 15 repetitions per set, however, would represent a good guideline. In order to complete that many repetitions, the resistance must be light so the possibility of injury or overexertion is minimal. Also, it is probably a good idea to decrease the number of sets and exercises you do. Two or three sets of an exercise for each muscle group is sufficient to provide the muscle with a suitable stimulus. There is absolutely no reason to do more unless you are interested in competitive lifting or bodybuilding.

The main focus of any training program, however, is consistency. No matter how much or how little you do, consistency will ensure some benefits. It is certainly much better to be consistently engaging in exercise than to be inconsistent or not exercising at all.

## MUSCLE RECOVERY WITH AGING

Unfortunately, aging muscle tissue loses some of its ability to recover. Although this is highly individualized, most lifelong weight trainers will attest to needing *more time* to *recover* from intense workouts and admit that their muscles just do not respond to a training stimulus as they did when they were younger. This phenomenon is very evident in the aging athlete who loses a step of his speed or timing and cannot continue putting forth intense efforts on a daily or weekly basis. Although many of these athletes maintain excellent skill and conditioning, it is not enough to keep them competitive at that level of play.

So, it is important, as you age, to take all of this into consideration when programming your workout. No one has to accept inactivity and boredom in later years. Fortunately, there are many people who are demonstrating that you can exercise throughout your lifetime and maintain an excellent physique. You may have to make some adjustments in your workouts (one hard workout every one to two weeks rather than every session), but the fact that you are out there exercising will place you well ahead of the average sedentary American in terms of fitness and physique. Although you can do little about the effects of aging on your facial features, you can do a lot toward having the body of someone years younger by engaging in a modest, consistent weight training program all of your life. It's never too late to start.

The loss of minerals from the skeletal system is known as _____ .

OSTEOPOROSIS

Which sex is more susceptible to osteoporosis with age, men or women?

WOMEN

Placing stresses on the skeletal system by contracting muscles (weight training) can _____ (HELP, HINDER) the structure and strength of bone.

HELP

The discs between the vertebrae in the spinal column act as _____ _____ when the spinal column is compressed.

SHOCK ABSORBERS

With aging, the discs lose some of their water content, making them more _____ and _____ .

RIGID, INFLEXIBLE

Exercising the spinal column _____ (CAN, CANNOT) help it endure the stresses that it incurs with aging.

CAN

There is approximately a 30 percent _____ (INCREASE, DECREASE) in muscle tissue throughout the course of one's adult life.

DECREASE

Weight training can have the effect of _____ (INCREASING, DECREASING) the loss of muscle tissue as one ages.

DECREASING

It _____ (IS, IS NOT) a natural phenomenon to put on weight with age.

IS NOT

The increase in body weight of aging people in Western cultures is more a function of overeating and _____.

INACTIVITY

Metabolism _____ _____ (SLOWS DOWN, SPEEDS UP) with age.

SLOWS DOWN

The decrease in metabolism with age means that the body needs _____ (MORE, FEWER) calories to maintain vital functions.

FEWER

It _____ (IS, IS NOT) possible to weigh the same as you age but increase your percentage of body fat.

IS

Since muscle is metabolically active at rest (burns calories), the more muscle you have, the (HIGHER, LOWER) your metabolic rate.

HIGHER

The real key to any training program throughout your lifetime is _____ no matter how much or little you do.

CONSISTENCY

---

# 18

# Designing Your Program—Guidelines

Chapter 2 covered the three training principles (tension, overload and specificity) that must be applied in attempting to increase strength. There are, however, many other guidelines and principles that you should be aware of in order to effectively design your own training program. The following addresses some of these issues and will help you establish some realistic goals and expectations concerning what you can accomplish from your training program.

## GETTING STARTED

The most important consideration in getting started is making sure you do not over-stress your muscles and end up with either extreme soreness or injury. For the first six to eight weeks, you need a program that will gradually condition your muscles and prepare them for the more intense work to follow. The heavier lifting and overload must come only after this initial period has passed.

Generally, a good beginning program should involve 12 to 15 repetitions per set for each major muscle group exercised. With this number of repetitions, the resistance has to be light, which decreases the possibility of straining your muscles. After the six- to eight-week conditioning period, you can adjust the resistance and repetitions in your program to more accurately reflect placing a true overload on your muscles.

As a beginner, your first few training sessions may have to be trial and error since you do not know which weight to use to perform 12 to 15 repetitions. If errors in judge-ment are to be made, however, it is best to err on the side of choosing too light a weight rather than one too heavy. You can always do more repetitions without injuring yourself if the weight is too light. However, if you choose a weight that is too heavy as a beginner, you greatly increase your chances of muscle soreness and injury.

It is unwise, as a beginning lifter, to overextend yourself during this initial condition-ing period. You should not feel overly sore or tight the day after your workout. If you do, you need to decrease the intensity in your next workout. As previously stated, your objective for this period should be to properly condition your muscles. Save your energy and enthusiasm for the more intense work that should follow this period.

For those people who prefer a more objective determination of starting weights, refer to Figure 18.1 for some examples. Notice that the starting weights are determined either by percentages of 1-RM or body weight. The problem with these determinations, however, is that a certain percentage of people will still have difficulty fitting into these parameters. The starting weights will be too much of an overload for some while not

## DETERMINING STARTING WEIGHTS

*Method A*

Body weight × percent = Starting weight
Example: 150 lbs. × 70% = 105 lbs. starting weight

*Method B*

One Rep Max × percent = Starting weight
Example: Bench press 110 lbs. × .70 = 77 lbs. starting weight

**Figure 18.1.** *Two ways to determine starting weights for the beginning lifter. Notice that both methods involve taking certain percentages of (a) one's body weight or (b) 1-RM.*

enough for others. They do, however, provide you with a good starting point that you can adjust as you discover your own strength potential.

## TRAINING PRINCIPLES

### Principle of Intensity (Sets and Repetitions)

When it comes to weight training, it is important to realize that there isn't one routine that is the best in terms of developing strength. Many studies have been conducted adjusting the number of sets, weight or repetitions, and most of them found no significant differences. Improvement in strength occurred with routines involving anywhere from one to six sets and from two to 10 repetitions in any combination. It is apparent that as long as a muscle is sufficiently overloaded, it will respond to a wide range of stimuli (sets and repetitions) by increasing strength.

A good basic routine to develop strength would involve performing three sets of an exercise and from six to 10 repetitions per set. Significant increases in strength, however, have occurred with routines involving six sets of 2 reps or 1 set of 10 reps. As a general rule, if you are going to do fewer repetitions per set (two to four), then you should do more sets (from three to six). If you do 10 or more repetitions per set, you can reduce the number of sets (from one to three).

### Principle of Change

It is a good idea to change your routine every three to four months to force your muscles to adapt to new and different stresses. This will ensure that they continue to increase in size and strength. It appears that, after a certain period of time, muscle has to be shocked or forced into developing greater strength and hypertrophy by being subjected to a different training routine. By selecting alternate exercises to work a muscle group, there is a different pattern of motor-unit activation and muscle fiber recruitment.

Consequently, muscle fibers that may not have been stressed previously are now activated and begin to increase in size. In addition to the physiological benefits of increased strength and hypertrophy, changing your routine every three to four months definitely has some psychological benefits as well. It is easy to get bored doing the same routine month after month. If you can look forward to a new routine, it keeps motivation, enthusiasm and energy levels high.

## Principle of Forced Repetitions

This is an important principle for beginning lifters who often fail to work out properly. It is important that, at least in one set, you complete as many repetitions as possible before putting the weights down. This type of set is referred to as forced repetitions or repetition maximum. If you always stop before feeling any discomfort or fatigue, you are probably compromising your potential for improving strength. Sometimes you must push yourself to ensure that you are properly stressing, or overloading, your muscles. By forcing out the last repetitions in a set, you can be certain that you are working hard enough to stimulate and encourage an increase in muscle strength and size.

Whenever you complete a workout, you should experience some degree of tightness or fatigue in your muscles. If they don't feel any different at the completion of a workout than they did at the beginning of it, you have probably not placed enough stress on your muscles. Many experienced lifters judge the performance of their workout simply by the tightness they feel in their muscles. The greater the tightness, the harder the workout. This tight feeling in the muscles is transitory and, depending upon the intensity of the workout, usually subsides within 15 to 30 minutes.

## Principle of Improvement

It is important to realize that improvement in strength will not progress at a constant rate or to the same degree with every individual. As a general rule, the greater the state of deconditioning, the greater the rate and magnitude of improvement that can be expected. Individuals close to their maximum strength will not improve as much or as quickly. The closer you progress towards your maximum strength potential, the more difficult it becomes to improve. Therefore, it is important to have realistic expectations concerning your improvement and to realize that much of it is dependent upon your initial level of strength.

## Principle of Strength Fluctuation

Your level of strength will fluctuate on a daily basis. Therefore, you shouldn't expect to equal or better your previous training performance every time you walk into a weight room. There will be days, sometimes even weeks, when you will not be able to lift as much weight. Factors such as stress, lack of sleep, poor nutrition, motivation, and fatigue, all affect strength. Beginning lifters may not experience this phenomenon quite as often as more seasoned lifters since they may be improving on a steady basis. At some point, however, progress will slow and these fluctuations in strength will occur.

On days when you are feeling strong, try to extend yourself somewhat and either lift a heavier weight or do more sets or repetitions. On days when you are feeling weak, reduce the intensity but do your workout. Even though you may not be able to lift as much, you can still put a decent stress on your muscles if you work up to your potential for that particular day. Remember, it is the tension generated in the muscles that counts, not necessarily how much weight you lift. If, by using a lighter weight and doing a few more repetitions you place the same stress on the muscle, the end result should be the same.

---

The primary consideration in starting a program is to make sure that you do not _____ your muscles so they end up sore or injured.

OVERSTRESS

The conditioning period should last anywhere from _____ to _____ weeks.

SIX, EIGHT

A good beginning routine is made up of how many repetitions per set?

12 to 15

To determine starting weight, you can use a percentage of a person's 1-RM or _____ _____ .

BODY WEIGHT

In terms of sets, researchers have found that anywhere from _____ to _____ are effective for developing strength.

ONE, SIX

In terms of repetitions, researchers have found that anywhere from _____ to _____ are effective for developing strength.

TWO, TEN

As a general rule, if you are going to do fewer reps (two to four) then you should do _____ (MORE, FEWER) sets and if you are going to do more reps (10 or more), you should do _____ (MORE, FEWER) sets.

MORE, FEWER

_____ repetitions for one set is a way of overloading a muscle.

FORCED

The more deconditioned you are when you start your training program, the _____ (GREATER, LESSER) the rate and magnitude of improvement you should expect.

GREATER

As you come closer to your maximum strength potential, it becomes _____ (EASIER, HARDER) to improve.

HARDER

You _____ (SHOULD, SHOULD NOT) expect to have the same level of strength every day.

SHOULD NOT

If you are feeling weak, you should continue your workout but _____ (INCREASE, DECREASE) the weights that you are using.

DECREASE

---

# COMPUTERIZED PROGRAMS

Weight training is an activity that can be easily programmed in terms of deciding how much weight should be attempted for each exercise. A daily, weekly or monthly schedule can be planned with specific goals. Recently, many computerized training programs have come on the market indicating how much a lifter should start with and how much weight to increase for each workout. It is important to understand that the programmer had to make many subjective decisions concerning how fast or slow beginning lifters improve their strength. At best, the schedule may reflect how the average beginning lifter could possibly improve on a week to week basis. But, for a myriad of reasons, many of which were addressed in the previous section (strength fluctuation), a computerized program can never replace the "computer" you have in your body giving you feedback on how you feel that day. If used as a general guideline rather than something that is absolute, however, computerized programs can be of some value to the beginning lifter.

## When to Increase Resistance

Whenever you are able to do more repetitions with the same weight, it is an indication that your muscles are ready for another overload. For example, if you started a set with 15 repetitions and, after a few weeks, are now able to do 20, it is time to increase the weight and bring the repetitions back down to 15 again. This process of overload and adaptation can continue until you reach a satisfactory level of strength. Whenever the weights you are working with start to feel light, you should consider increasing the resistance.

## Principle of Adaptation

If there were no adaptation to the stresses placed on your muscles through resistive exercises, there would be absolutely no reason to train with weights. The increase in strength and size with training is due to neuromuscular (motor-unit recruitment) and physical (increase in protein filaments) changes that occur in muscle. Generally speaking, you can expect your muscles to adapt to the stresses you place on them within two to four weeks. The reason for the wide variance is simply that some peoples' systems respond or adapt much quicker than others. Also to be considered is the conditioning level of the lifter. The better one's condition, the longer the period for improvement. It is not unusual for the beginning lifter to make strength gains of 2 to 5 percent per week. That same percent improvement for the more advanced lifter may take anywhere from several weeks to several months.

It is important to realize that not all muscles will adapt at the same rate or in the same manner. Some muscles will increase in strength and size quite readily while others will respond much slower and with much less hypertrophy. Body builders can tell you of at least one muscle group that will not hypertrophy no matter how hard they work it. Some have even gone as far as injecting steroids into specific muscles to induce them to grow, but with little success. Although the answer to this phenomenon has yet to be explained, it appears that genetics (heredity) is a major factor. If you resist your natural tendencies (you're basically thin but want to be heavily muscled), your muscles may not respond as you desire no matter how hard you try. You will definitely grow stronger from the training, but you may not get the hypertrophy that you were anticipating.

## Principle of Rest Between Sets

Generally speaking, the heavier the weight you are working with, the longer the recovery needed between sets. Conversely, the lighter the weight, the less time needed for recovery before starting another set or exercise. In terms of time, the rest interval can be anywhere from one to two minutes for lighter sets to about three to five minutes for heavier sets. It is not unusual for competitive power lifters to rest five to 10 minutes between sets. Since they are working with weights very close to their maximums, it is necessary for their muscles to be fully recovered before beginning another set. Rest intervals of *one* to *three* minutes, however, should be sufficient for most recreational lifters.

## Principle of Working Large Muscles First

In determining the order of exercises in your program, it is important to work the large muscle groups of the chest and back before doing exercises to isolate the smaller muscles in the arms. Since the larger muscles of the chest and back cannot be exercised without using the arms, it is important to make sure that the arm muscles are not fatigued. If they are, it will compromise the overload that can be placed on the chest and back, thus limiting their development.

Exercises that involve more than one major muscle group are referred to as complex, while exercises that work only one major muscle group are referred to as isolations. All of the complex exercises for a specific muscle group should be done before doing any isolation exercises. Figure 18.2 provides examples of complex and isolation exercises.

As a general rule, you should work the muscles on your thorax (chest and back) and your shoulders before working your arms. In addition, you should always do your presses before doing isolations on your shoulders and chest. Examples of these situations are provided in Figure 18.3. Figure 18.4 illustrates a good way to organize a general training program in terms of order. Notice that the more complex and large muscle group exercises are listed before the smaller muscle groups. The legs should follow a similar pattern, with the presses and squats coming before the extensions and curls. It really doesn't matter whether you work your legs before or after you exercise your upper body since fatiguing them will not impact your upper body workout.

| COMPLEX | | ISOLATIONS | |
|---|---|---|---|

COMPLEX

Bench press
Decline press    Chest
Incline press
Push-ups

Military press    Shoulder
Upright rows

Lat pulldowns
Seated rows          Lats
Bent-over rows      (Midback)
Pull-ups

Bent-over rows
Lat pulldowns             Trapezius
Behind head pull-ups    (Upper Back)
Behind head military
   press

Dead lift    Erector Spinae
             (Lower Back)

Squat     Quadriceps
Leg Press  (Front Thigh
Lunges     and Legs)

Dips
Narrow grip bench    Triceps
   press             (Back Arm)

Narrow grip pull-ups    Biceps
Upright rows            (Front Arm)

ISOLATIONS

Flys
Cable crossovers    Chest

Front raises—dumbbell
Lateral raises—dumbbell          Shoulder
Bent-over raises—dumbbell

One arm pull in—    Lats
   dumbbell         (Midback)

Shoulder shrugs    Trapezius
                   (Upper Back)

Hyperextensions    Erector Spinae
Good mornings      (Lower Back)

Knee extension    Quadriceps
                  (Front Thigh)

Leg curl    Hamstring
            (Back Thigh)

Toe raises    "Gastroc"
              (Calf)

Toe curls    Tibia Anterior
             (Front of Leg)

Extensions    Tricep
              (Back Arm)

Curls    Biceps
         (Front Arm)

Wrist curls    Flexors (Forearms)

Wrist extensions    Extensors
                    (Forearms)

**Figure 18.2.** *A listing of both complex and isolation muscle group exercises. You should arrange your program so you are doing the larger muscle group exercises (complex) before isolating and focusing on the smaller muscle group exercises (isolations).*

CHEST                           SHOULDERS
COMPLEX                         COMPLEX

1. Bench press                  1. Military press
2. Incline press                2. Upright rows
3. Decline press
4. Narrow-grip bench press
5. Push ups

ISOLATIONS                      ISOLATIONS

6. Flys                         3. Front dumbbell raise
7. Incline flys                 4. Lateral dumbbell raise
8. Decline flys                 5. Bent-over raise
9. Cable cross-overs

*Figure 18.3. Examples of how to arrange exercises from the more complex presses to the more focused isolations for the chest and shoulders.*

1. Bench press (c)              14. Dips (c)            Triceps
2. Incline press (c)  Chest     15. Tricep extensions (i)
3. Flys (i)
                                16. Wrist curls (i)        Forearm
4. Military press (c)           17. Wrist extensions (i)
5. Upright rows (c)   Shoulder
6. Lateral raises (i)           18. Dead lift (c)        Lower Back
                                19. Hyperextensions (i)
7. Pull-ups (c)
8. Lat pulldowns (c)            20. Squats (c)
9. Seated rows (c)      Lats    21. Lunges (c)              Quadriceps
10. Bent-over rows (c)          22. Leg press (c)
11. One arm pull in (i)         23. Knee extensions (i)

12. Shoulder shrugs (i)   Trapezius   24. Leg curls (i)   Hamstrings

13. Bicep curls (i)   Biceps    25. Toe raises (i)   Calf

                                26. Toe curls (i)   Tibialis Anterior

*Figure 18.4. An example of how to organize the order of exercises that you would perform in your routine. Notice that the larger muscle group exercises are listed first. This is done to ensure that these muscles will get a proper stress without being limited by fatigue from the smaller muscle groups.*

## Principle of Muscle Balance

It is important that you design your program so it does not result in an imbalance of strength between opposing muscle groups. Anatomically, the human body is designed very simply. If a muscle group does a certain action on the front side of the body, muscles on the opposite, or back, side of the body will do the opposite action. It is important, then, that you work both muscle groups equally so they can counterbalance each other. If one muscle group is significantly stronger than the other, the chances of injuring the weaker muscle group becomes much greater. Figure 18.5 provides a list of opposing muscle groups and their actions.

## Principle of Recovery (Frequency)

There is absolutely no question that you have to allow adequate time for your muscles to recover between workouts. If this is not provided, the possibility of injury increases while the ability of the muscle to generate force decreases. It is apparent that the muscle-synthesizing, or building, process takes time to occur. By not allowing your muscles sufficient time to recover, the only thing that will happen is a breakdown of tissue. Depending upon the intensity of the workout, it takes anywhere from 24 to 48 hours for the muscle to be fully recovered.

| MUSCLE | ACTION | MUSCLE | ACTION |
|---|---|---|---|
| Biceps | (flexes arm) | Triceps | (extends arm) |
| Forearm flexors | (flexes wrist) | Forearm extensors | (extends wrist) |
| Shoulder "Deltoid" | (raises arm) | "Lats" | (lowers arm) |
| Chest "Pectorals" | (adducts arm) | Middle Trapezius Posterior Deltoid | (abducts arm) |
| Abdomen "Rectus Abdominus" | (flexes trunk) | Erector Spinae | (extends trunk) |
| Hip flexors "Pseab major" | (flexes hip) | Buttocks "Gluteals" | (extends hip) |
| Front thigh "Quadriceps" | (extends knee) | Back thigh "Hamstring" | (flexes knee) |
| Tibialis Anterior | (flexes foot) | Calf "Gastroc" | (extends foot) |

**Figure 18.5.** *A list of muscles that oppose each other and their actions in the body. It is important to exercise opposing groups equally since a muscle imbalance could lead to potential injury.*

**Figure 18a.** *Most body builders who work out six days per week split their routine so they are not working the same muscle group two days in a row.*

For the recreational lifter, a routine performed two to three times a week is sufficient. Research has demonstrated this to be an adequate frequency in terms of developing strength and allowing time for muscle recovery. Although strength can be maintained but not increased with a one-day-per-week workout, it is not recommended since the chance of injury and soreness is much greater when lifting so infrequently. On the other hand, performing the same routine more than three times per week does not allow the muscle adequate recovery time.

It is not uncommon for body builders to lift six days a week, however, they do not work the same muscle groups each day. This is called a "split routine" and is designed to provide the muscles with sufficient rest. Figure 18.6 illustrates a good example of a six-day split routine. Notice that certain muscle groups are worked together on one day while certain other groups are worked on other days. The reason is that these muscle groups usually work in combination with each other. For example, in exercising the chest, several exercises such as the bench press, incline press and decline press also involve the shoulder and tricep muscle. Consequently, since they are already being exercised, it makes sense to include them with your chest workout. The bicep muscle is involved with the lats in

## SIX DAY SPLIT ROUTINE

| DAYS OF THE WEEK | MUSCLE GROUPS |
| --- | --- |
| Monday/Thursday | Chest<br>Shoulders<br>Triceps<br>Forearm extensors |
| Tuesday/Friday | Lats<br>Biceps<br>Forearm flexors |
| Wednesday/Saturday | Quadriceps<br>Hamstring<br>Gluteals (Buttocks)<br>Calf<br><br>*Trapezius—This is a very difficult muscle to work. It is primarily involved in Lat and Shoulder work. |

**Figure 18.6.** *An example of a six-day split routine. Notice that each major muscle group gets two days of rest even though the individual is lifting six days. If you are planning on lifting more than three times per week, it is almost imperative that you split your routine to allow for muscle recovery and synthesis.*

performing any pulling motion; therefore, it is included on the day that the lats are worked. Notice that every major muscle group is worked twice a week with adequate recovery time provided between each workout.

As a general rule, you should increase the resistances you are working with when you can do _____ (MORE, FEWER) repetitions in a set.

MORE

If you initially started off with 10 reps in a set, you should increase the weight and bring the reps back down to 10 when you get to _____ reps.

15

The trouble with a computerized program is that it can't tell you how you are _____ that particular day.

FEELING

Muscle _____ (DOES, DOES NOT) adapt at the same rate even within the same individual.

DOES NOT

Generally speaking, the heavier the weight you are working out with, the _____ (LONGER, SHORTER) the recovery time should be between sets.

LONGER

An average recovery period between sets would be anywhere from _____ to _____ minutes.

ONE, THREE

In determining the order of exercises in your program, you should always do those that involve the _____ (LARGER, SMALLER) muscle groups first.

LARGER

As a general rule, you should always do exercises for your _____ and _____ (CHEST, BACK, ARMS) before doing exercises for your _____ (CHEST, BACK, ARMS).

CHEST/BACK, ARMS

If you develop an imbalance between opposing muscle groups, the chances of injuring the _____ (STRONGER, WEAKER) muscle group becomes much greater.

WEAKER

The muscles on one side of the body do one action while the muscles on the _____ side of the body do the _____ action.

OPPOSITE/OPPOSITE

Generally speaking, it takes anywhere from _____ to _____ hours for your muscles to recover from a previous workout.

24, 48

A _____ routine means that you exercise different body parts on different days.

SPLIT

---

# 19

# Designing Your Program—Routines

Now that you have been introduced to the various physiological principles and concepts, it is time to focus upon designing your weight training program utilizing these parameters. Of course it is important that you have a goal in mind for training with weights. Once that goal is identified, the routine you design will be the means that will allow you to accomplish that end.

Obviously, people who train with weights to become body builders or competitive athletes will design a much more intense and extensive routine than someone interested in only gaining a minimal amount of strength and good muscle tone. As you learned in Chapter 18, there is no "one best" routine. As long as you are creating tension and overloading your muscles properly, they will respond by becoming stronger and more defined regardless of the routine that you use. Some routines may be more effective than others in developing strength or hypertrophy, but the bottom line is the amount of work that you do in the weight room. The more work you do, the greater the benefits.

The following information is provided for you to use as a guideline in designing your own weight training program. It is, by necessity, basic and unspecific but, for the recreational lifter, it will be more than adequate in terms of providing you with a solid foundation that you can adapt and modify to your own needs.

## General Routine

A good general routine should include all of the major muscle groups in the body (lower as well as upper). As you can see in Figure 19.1, this does not involve an extraordinary number of muscles. If you do at least one exercise for each muscle group and complete two to three sets, that should be sufficient in terms of developing adequate strength and tone for the average recreational lifter.

Figure 19.2 provides you with a list of several different exercises that work each of the major muscle groups. The descriptions of these exercises are located in Chapter 20. Your routine can include one or several of these exercises for each muscle group, depending upon your specific goals and objectives. It is not a bad idea to alternate exercises every three to four months. By doing this, you are ensuring that your muscles will develop more completely. Of course, if you are trying to work on one body part in particular, you will probably want to focus on doing as many different exercises for that body part as possible. The more ways you exercise a muscle, the better chance you have of developing it more fully.

| COMMON NAME | TECHNICAL NAME |
|---|---|
| Chest | Pectoralis Major—pectorals |
| Shoulder | Deltoid |
| Arm | Biceps (Front) <br> Triceps (Back) |
| Forearm | Flexors (Palm side of hand) <br> Extensors (Back side of hand) |
| Upper back | Trapezius—traps |
| Mid-back | Latissimus Dorsi—lats |
| Lower back | Erector Spinae |
| Stomach | Rectus Abdomins—abdominals, abs |
| Buttocks | Gluteus Maximus—gluteals |
| Thigh | Quadriceps (Front) <br> Hamstrings (Back) |
| Calf | Gastrocnemius—gastroc (Back) <br> Tibialis Anterior (Front) |

**Figure 19.1.** *A listing of the major muscle groups, including common and technical names. These 15 muscles are responsible for most of the major movements in the body.*

## ESTABLISHING A ROUTINE

Once you have selected the exercises you want to include in your routine and have made sure that you are working every major muscle group, the next step is to put them into some logical order of progression. Figure 19.3 provides you with an example of how to order the exercises in a routine from the more complex to the isolations (exercises that work only one muscle group). As you can see, the muscles on the thorax (chest cavity) involving the presses and pulls are more complex than some of the other exercises that isolate on the specific muscle groups such as the flys (chest), dumbbell raises (shoulders), curls (biceps) and extensions (triceps).

After you have figured out the order of the exercises, you need to decide what type of training system you are going to use for those exercises. Again, depending upon your

# SPECIFIC EXERCISES FOR EACH MAJOR MUSCLE GROUP

CHEST—Pectorals

- Bench press
- Push-ups
- Incline press
- Decline press
- Cable crossovers
- Flys
- Pullovers

SHOULDERS—Deltoid

- Military press
- Behind the head press
- Upright rowing
- Front dumbbell raise
- Lateral dumbbell raise
- Bent-over dumbbell raise

UPPER BACK—Trapezius

- Shoulder shrug
- Upright rowing
- Behind the head press
- Bent-over dumbbell raise

MID-BACK—Lats

- Lat pulldowns
- Pull-ups
- Chin-ups
- Bent-over rowing
- Seated rowing
- One arm dumbbell pull-in

FRONT ARM—Biceps

- Curls—variations
- Pull-ups

BACK OF ARM—Triceps

- Dips
- Close grip bench press
- Extensions (pulley machine)

FOREARM

- Wrist curls (Flexors)
- Wrist extensions (Extensors)

LOWER BACK—Erector Spinae

- Back extensions
- Dead lift
- Good mornings

BUTTOCKS—Gluteals

- Deep squats
- Lunges

FRONT THIGH—Quadriceps

- Squat
- Leg press (machine)
- Knee extension (machine)
- Lunges

BACK THIGH—Hamstring

- Hamstring curls (machine)

CALF—Gastroc

- Toe raises
- Calf raises (machine)

**Figure 19.2.** *A listing of specific exercises that work each of the major muscle groups in the body. Notice that some exercises work more than one major muscle group.*

specific goals and objectives, all or some of these systems of training can be incorporated, at some point, into your program. Again, it is beneficial to change your routine or training system every so often so the muscles do not get used to a specific training pattern.

|     |                          |                            |
| --- | ------------------------ | -------------------------- |
| 1.  | Bench press (c)          | Chest                      |
| 2.  | Flys (i)                 | Chest                      |
| 3.  | Military press (c)       | Shoulders                  |
| 4.  | Upright rowing (c)       | Shoulders/Trapezius        |
| 5.  | Front dumbbell raises (i)| Shoulders                  |
| 6.  | Behind the head press (c)| Trapezius (Upper Back)     |
| 7.  | Shoulder shrugs (i)      | Trapezius (Upper Back)     |
| 8.  | Pull-ups (c)             | Lats (Mid-back)            |
| 9.  | Seated Rowing (c)        | Lats (Mid-back)            |
| 10. | Back extensions (i)      | Erector Spinae (Lower Back)|
| 11. | Bicep curl (i)           | Front arm—Biceps           |
| 12. | Dips (i)                 | Back arm—Triceps           |
| 13. | Wrist curl (i)           | Palm side of forearm       |
| 14. | Wrist extension (i)      | Back side of forearm       |
| 15. | Squat (c)                | Quadriceps (Front Thigh)   |
| 16. | Lunges (c)               | Gluteals/Quadriceps        |
| 17. | Knee extensions (i)      | Quadriceps (Front Thigh)   |
| 18. | Hamstring curls (i)      | Hamstrings (Back Thigh)    |
| 19. | Toe raises (i)           | Gastroc (Calf)             |

**Figure 19.3.** *A typical routine showing how the order of exercises proceeds from the more complex (c) to isolations (i) and the larger muscle groups to smaller ones. For illustrative purposes, more than one exercise was included for each muscle group; however, for the beginner, it would not be necessary to do more than one exercise per muscle group.*

## PERIODIZATION

This concept is used mostly with competitive athletic programs. It can, however, have practical application for anyone training with weights. Essentially, periodization involves breaking the year down into specific periods (usually four) with different training or strength goals identified within each period (Figure 19.4). Obviously, with different goals, the routines or intensity of lifting will be different. For example, during the athlete's season, the major objective of the weight training program is to maintain the strength that was developed during the off season. Consequently, the athlete would lift moderately heavy weights but would cut down on the number of sets and days and would keep the repetitions somewhat high. During the off season, the major objective is to improve strength significantly. Therefore, the athlete would lift heavier weights and do fewer reps while increasing the number of sets and days that he would workout.

It is not a bad idea for the recreational athlete to follow a similar pattern. During one period, you could work on improving strength, while in another period you could work on muscle endurance. It is virtually impossible to try to increase strength on a continuing basis year in and year out. There are going to be inevitable peaks and valleys. Periodization is one method of planning these changes in a structured, systematic way.

## PERIODIZATION

|  |  | GOAL | INTENSITY | ROUTINE | DAYS |
|---|---|---|---|---|---|
| Period 1 | **Immediate Postseason** | Conditioning | Moderate | 2-3 sets 8-12 reps | 2-3 days |
| Period 2 | **Off season** | Strength | Very high | 3-5 sets 4-8 reps | 3-4 days |
| Period 3 | **Preseason** | Strength/ Flexibility | High | 3 sets 6-10 reps | 3 days |
| Period 4 | **In season** | Maintenance | Moderate | 1-2 sets 8-15 reps | 1-2 days |

**Figure 19.4.** *A hypothetical periodization training program for an athlete trying to improve his strength. Notice for different periods there are different training goals and routines. The hardest work and greatest gains should be programmed during the off season.*

## TRAINING SYSTEMS

The following training systems are simply different techniques that you can apply to your basic routine. Again, it warrants repeating that any of these systems are effective as long as you are creating tension in your muscles. You may like some systems more than others and decide to incorporate one or two into your training routine. It wouldn't hurt, however, to experiment with as many of them as possible and see how your body responds to each one.

The following training systems are some of the most common and will give you some idea of how you can vary your routine to obtain your goals. It is by no means complete, but it is certainly adequate for the beginning lifter in terms of providing some idea of the options available for a basic routine.

### Set System

The set system is the basis for any training routine. Basically all of the systems included in this section are variations of the set system. In this system, you perform a certain amount of repetitions of an exercise, then rest. This constitutes one set. If you are going to do three sets of an exercise, you would repeat this process two more times. It is common practice to keep the weight and repetitions the same in this system. In communicating the set system, 3 × 10 at 80 would represent three sets of 10 repetitions at 80 pounds. Most routines are written in this manner.

## Circuit Training System

A circuit is simply a routine designed so you move from one exercise to another in a determined pattern. You usually do one set at each exercise or station until the circuit is complete, then repeat the circuit one or more times to get an additional overload. It is possible, however, to do several sets at one station before moving on to the next one. As long as the same amount of work is done in each circuit, the same benefits will accrue. Circuit training is advantageous when used with large groups because it allows everyone to get the same workout in a relatively short period of time. Timed circuits, which include a certain interval for exercise, another for recovery and another for changing stations, also works well for large groups when time is a factor.

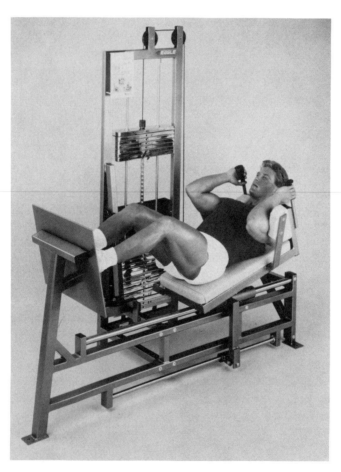

**Figure 19a.** *By changing body position, this quadricep exercise reduces the stress imposed upon the back. Courtesy of* **CYBEX**/*Eagle Fitness Systems.*

## Light-to-Heavy System

In this system, you increase the weight whenever you do another set. The repetitions can either remain the same or decrease with the increase in weight. For example, if the reps were to remain constant, a light-to-heavy system for one exercise might look like this: 3 × 10 at 30, 40 and 50 pounds. If the reps were to decrease, the three sets might look like this: 1 × 10 at 30; 1 × 8 at 40; 1 × 6 at 50. The advantage of using the light-to-heavy system is that your first couple of sets are actually a warm-up, minimizing the possibility of injuring yourself when you get to your heaviest set. A disadvantage of this system is the possibility your muscles could become fatigued with the earlier sets, thereby limiting your ability to perform the last set that represents the true overload.

## Heavy-to-Light System

This is the opposite of the light-to-heavy system but offers the advantage of lifting the heaviest weight when you are fresh and not fatigued. The disadvantage, however, is that you are not warmed up and could injure yourself attempting the first set. With this system, it is imperative that you warm up properly before lifting. A good five to 10 minutes of stationary bicycle riding, calisthenics or rope jumping should be adequate. A typical heavy-to-light system might look like this: 3 × 10 at 50, 40 and 30 pounds if the reps are kept constant, or 1 × 6 at 50; 1 × 8 at 40; and 1 × 10 at 30 if the reps are increased. Many students have indicated that they get a more intense workout with this system over the light-to-heavy system. Apparently, once the muscle gets fatigued doing the first heavy set, the next two sets are difficult even though the weight is being decreased.

## Pyramid System

This system is most commonly used as a combination of both the light-to-heavy and heavy-to-light systems. The lifter will start out light-to-heavy, increasing the weights while decreasing the reps until he gets to his heaviest weight and then usually come back down, heavy-to-light, decreasing the weight while increasing the number of reps. This system is very effective in terms of developng strength and muscle hypertrophy since it places a significant stress on the muscles during those last sets. Of course, it takes more time since you are doing a minimum of five sets for each exercise (two on the way up, then the overload and two on the way down).

## One Set to Failure

This is a good system to consider if time is a factor. Ideally, you should try to do anywhere from eight to 15 repetitions in a slow, controlled manner, forcing out the last couple of repetitions until you absolutely cannot do anymore. With this technique, you are ensured of placing an adequate overload on the muscle and getting the most from the one set that you are doing for each muscle group.

## Slow Rep System

With this system, you lift very slowly, trying to minimize the effects momentum has on the resistance you are moving. Remember, it is tension that you are trying to create in the muscle. Momentum (swinging of the weights) generates very little tension once the weights are in motion. Consequently, if you lift slowly, you will find that it creates much more tension in the muscle throughout the entire range of motion (ROM). The only drawback to this type of system is that you have to use lighter weights than normal since it would be impossible to complete the ROM with heavier weights. As a general rule, you should take from two to three seconds for the concentric phase of the contraction (the push or pull phase) and four to six seconds for the eccentric phase of the contraction (resisting the push or pull phase). You only need to do one to two sets of each exercise utilizing this technique.

### Aerobic System

With this system, you proceed from one exercise to the other (circuit training) with very little rest. You usually set up this circuit so you are working a different body part (arms then legs, chest then back) at each station. This will allow you to move from one exercise to another very rapidly since the same muscles are not worked twice in a row. A typical system might consist of 45 seconds of exercise (fairly rapid reps) and 15 seconds of recovery with the whole workout lasting approximately 30 minutes. Obviously, with this system you have to use very light resistances in order to allow time for your muscles to recover and complete the circuit. A variation of this system is to include some type of aerobic exercise (stationary bicycling, rope jumping, jogging in place, calisthenics, etc.) for 45 to 60 seconds between each exercise. Obviously, this would enhance the aerobic bene-fits of the circuit significantly. It is important to note that with this system, because you are using relatively light weights, you are compromising on the amount of strength that could be developed. If, however, you don't have the time to do both an aerobic and weight training workout, a system such as this would be sufficient in terms of developing a minimal amount of aerobic endurance and muscle strength.

### Super Set System

A super set involves doing two exercises in succession without resting. The first exercise works one muscle group (prime mover), while the second works the antagonist or opposing muscle group. Figure 19.5 provides a list of prime mover and opposing muscle groups that you could combine into a super set routine. Super setting the arms is particu-larly effective because you will be able to feel them getting tighter in response to working both bicep and tricep muscle groups. Doing super sets is also a good way to consolidate time since you are essentially exercising two muscle groups together and resting half as much.

### Burn, or Continuous Set, System

I like to refer to this system as the burn system because that is exactly what you will feel in your muscles after completing a set. Essentially, this is a heavy-to-light system but without the rest between sets. After completing one set at a given weight, you reduce the weight immediately and do another set of as many reps as possible. You continue in this manner, reducing weight and doing as many reps as possible, until you have completely fatigued the muscle (from three to six sets). Since you are not giving your muscle ade-

## OPPOSING MUSCLE GROUPS

Chest (Pectorals)—Mid-back (Lats)

Front arm (Biceps)—Back arms (Triceps)

Wrist flexors—Wrist extensors

Abdomen—Lower back

Buttocks (Gluteals)—Hip Flexors

Front thigh (Quadriceps)—Back thigh (Hamstrings)

Front calf (Tibialis Anterior)—Back calf (Gastroc)

**Figure 19.5.** *A list of opposing muscle groups for super setting. Doing super sets saves time and is an effective way to work the arms and legs.*

quate time to recover, you will find the last sets extremely difficult and sometimes painful, although you are working with lighter weights. This system is a good one to use occasionally to shock your muscles and to get a good "pump" (tight feeling).

## Split System

As discussed in Chapter 18, you would use a split system of training when you are planning to work out more than three times a week. Working the same muscle group every day would eventually lead to muscle fatigue and injury. You should do all of your presses and pushes on one day, all of your pulls and curls on the second and your legs on the third. This routine ensures that you are working compatible muscle groups on the same days, thus allowing for adequate recovery of the muscles before they are stressed again. Figure 18.6 in Chapter 18 provides you with a basic six-day split routine.

# 20

# Exercises

This final chapter describes some of the more basic exercises that work the major muscle groups of the body. It is designed to help you understand how the muscle is situated in the body, what action it is responsible for when it contracts or shortens, and what movements or exercises will develop it. For the beginner, the exercises included in this chapter are more than adequate in terms of developing each muscle group. For those individuals desiring more specific exercises, however, there are many excellent body building books on the market to serve that purpose.

Basically, muscles move our body because they are attached to our skeletal system in such a way that, when they contract, they exert a force on bones and pull one toward the other. If you know how the muscles are attached to the skeletal system and also know in which direction the fibers lie, you can determine the action of the muscle (Figure 20.1). Strengthening a muscle involves performing the *action* of that muscle against a resistance.

## BASIC MOVEMENTS OF THE BODY

Although there are many other movements of the skeletal system, in this book, we will concentrate only on the basic four, which include flexion, extension, abduction and adduction. As you can see in Figure 20.2, *flexion* is simply the bending of a joint so the angle between the bones decreases. *Extension* is the opposite action: straightening of a joint so the angle between the bones increases. Bringing your hand up to your shoulder involves flexion (bending) of the elbow while returning it to the starting position involves elbow extension. *Abduction* is simply any movement away from the midline of the body. *Adduction* is any movement toward the midline of the body. Moving your arms out from your sides is abduction; returning them to the starting position constitutes adduction. With these four movements, you should have a fairly good understanding of most of the movements of the major muscle groups.

The remainder of the chapter is organized in the following manner: For each muscle group, the general location on the skeletal system, fiber direction and action will be given. In addition, illustrations will show how the muscle is situated on the skeletal system both in isolation and with other surrounding muscle groups. Finally, the exercises that work that particular muscle group will be presented. Hopefully, this organization will help you understand why you do certain exercises to develop certain muscle groups.

### Primary/Secondary Muscle Involvement

You will notice that many of the exercises develop more than one muscle group. It is important to keep in mind that the first muscle group listed is the primary one responsible

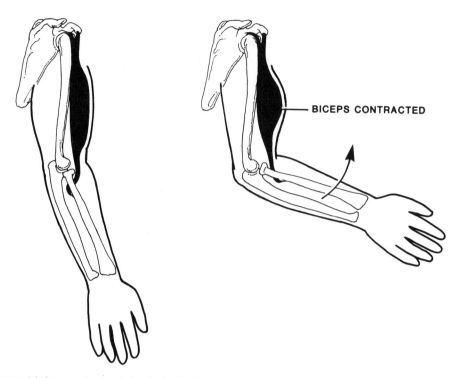

**BICEPS CONTRACTED**

**Figure 20.1.** *The bicep muscle is attached at the shoulder (origin) and below the elbow (insertion). Since the insertion is the movable part, when the muscle contracts, it will flex or bend the elbow.*

for the movement and the one that gets most of the stress and benefit. The secondary muscle groups get some benefit because they either stabilize a body part or assist the primary muscle group in the movement. In many instances, the amount of weight you can lift in a certain exercise is determined by the strength in the muscle groups that are assisting the primary mover. For example, weak triceps (back of the arm) may be a limiting factor in how much weight you can successfully lift in the bench press. Although you may be able to get the weight easily off your chest, your triceps may not be able to extend or straighten your arms.

## Origin/Insertion

Note that the origin and insertion for each muscle group is given in general, rather than specific, terms. It serves no useful purpose to get so technical in a book for beginners. The *origin* is always the part of the muscle that is stabilized, the *insertion*, the part that will move when the muscle contracts. As long as you are aware of the general areas of the origin and insertion, you should be able to figure out the action of the muscle.

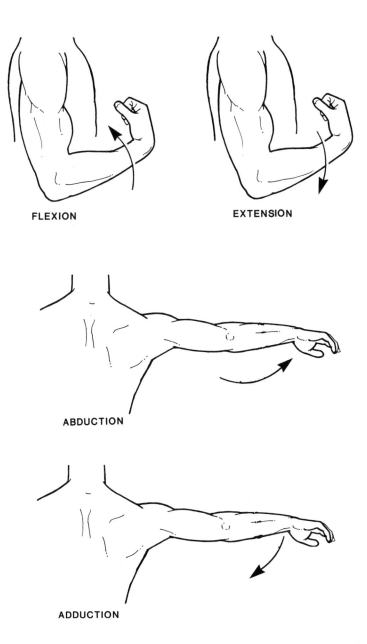

**FLEXION**

**EXTENSION**

**ABDUCTION**

**ADDUCTION**

**Figure 20.2.** *The four basic movements of the body, (a) flexion, (b) extension, (c) abduction, and (d) adduction. The actions of the major muscle groups usually involve one of these four movements.*

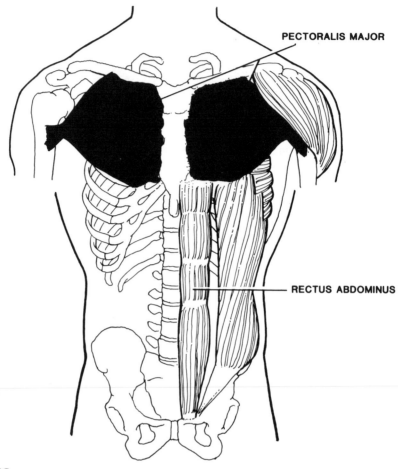

PECTORALIS MAJOR

RECTUS ABDOMINUS

## EXERCISES

### Chest—Pectoralis Major (Pectorals)

Origin—sternum or breastbone of the rib cage
Insertion—upper arm
Fiber Direction—horizontal
Action—adduction of the arm, pulls arm in toward the midline of body

### Exercises for the Chest

**Bench Press** (develops the *middle chest*, anterior deltoid-shoulder, triceps)
Important points:
1. Wrap your thumbs around the bar for safety and get an even grip (approximately shoulder-width apart).
2. Keep your back flat on the bench, feet on the floor, do not arch your back or wiggle to complete the lift.

CONCENTRIC

3. Don't bounce the bar off your chest, bring it down slowly and with control.
4. Bring the bar down to your lower chest and lock out at the finish (arms completely extended).
5. Always use a spotter and collars with a free bar.
6. Exhale as you push the bar up.

**Incline Press** (develops the *upper chest*, anterior deltoid-shoulder, triceps)
Important points:
1. Same points for bench press.
2. Keep your arms comfortably above your head. Do not hold them in a position that requires you to exert force to keep them up.

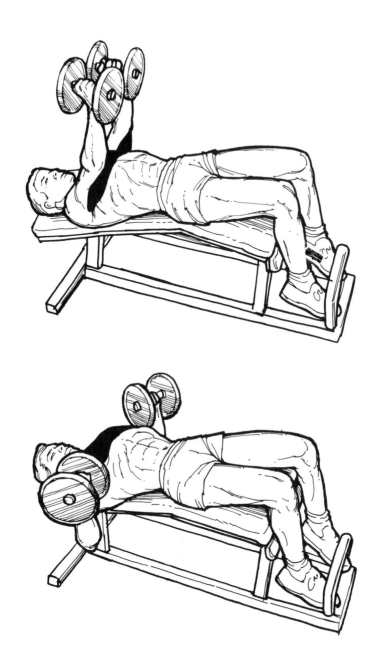

**Decline Press** (develops the *lower chest*, triceps)
Important points:
1. Same points for bench and incline press.

**Flys** (develops the middle chest)

Important points:

1. Use an arcing motion (half circle) down and back up.
2. It is acceptable to bend your elbows as long as you come back up in an arc and not a push. Keeping your elbows straight may strain that joint.
3. The focus should be on stretching the chest muscle, not on keeping the arms straight.
4. Flys can also be done on an incline or decline bench.
5. Exhale as you bring the arms back to the starting position.

**Pullovers** (chest expander)

Important points:

1. Try to stretch out behind you as much as possible.
2. It is acceptable to bend your elbows, but try to focus on stretching the chest.
3. Use an arcing motion (half circle) with your arms.
4. Keep arms straight up over the chest at the start and finish of the movement.
5. Exhale as you bring the weight back to the starting position.

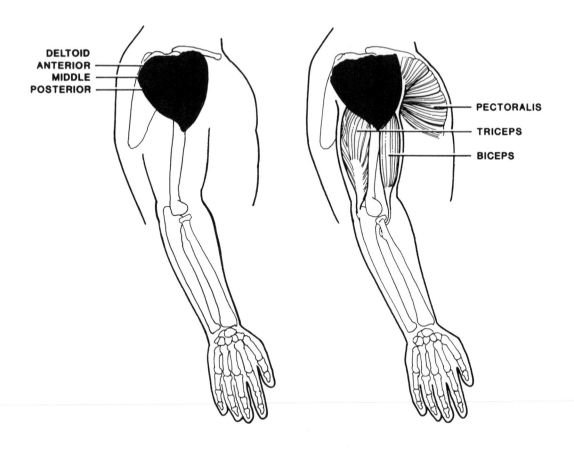

DELTOID
ANTERIOR
MIDDLE
POSTERIOR

PECTORALIS

TRICEPS

BICEPS

## Shoulders—(Deltoid: Anterior, Middle, Posterior)

Origin—top of the shoulder
Insertion—upper arm
Fiber Direction—vertical
Action—abduction of the arm, moves arm up and out to the side

### Exercises for the Shoulders

**Military Press** (develops the *middle deltoid*, trapezius, triceps)
Important points:
1. People with lower back problems should avoid this exercise.
2. Try to lift with a flat back—do not arch excessively.
3. Use a shoulder-width grip and extend or lock out your arms fully.
4. Exhale as you push the weight up.

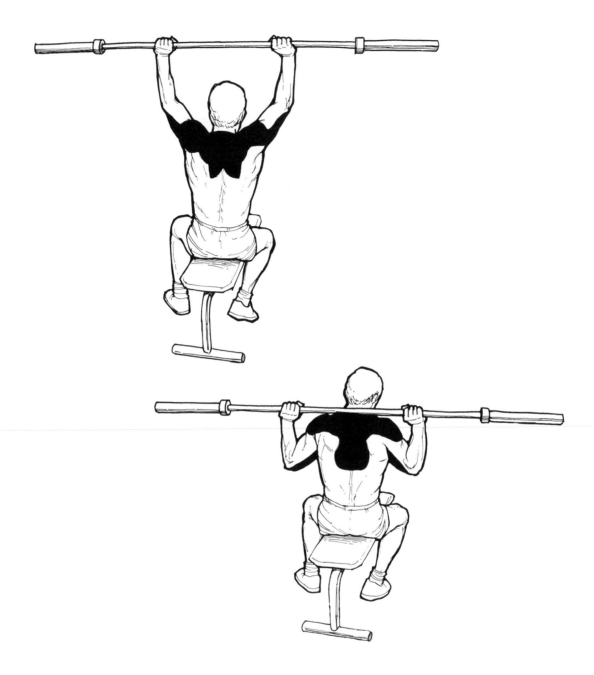

**Behind the Head Press** (develops the *middle deltoid*, trapezius, triceps)
Important points:
1. Same as for military press; places a little more stress on the trapezius.
2. Grip should be slightly wider than shoulder-width.

**Upright Rowing** (develops the *middle deltoid*, trapezius, biceps)
Important points:
1. Remember to keep your elbows higher than the bar and use a narrow grip.
2. Pull the bar up under your chin.
3. Inhale as you pull up.

**Front Dumbbell Raise** (develops the *anterior deltoid*, trapezius)

Important points:

1. Alternate arms: One goes up as the other returns to the starting position.
2. Palms can either be facing down or inward.
3. Elbows can be slightly bent. Straight arms may eventually cause elbow strain.
4. Bring weights to shoulder height, then return to starting position.

**Lateral Dumbbell Raise** (develops the *middle deltoid*, trapezius)
Important points:
1. Bring arms from your sides up to shoulder height.
2. It is acceptable to bend your elbows slightly as you bring the weights up.
3. Exhale as you lower the dumbbells to the starting position.

**Bent-Over Dumbbell Raise** (develops the *posterior deltoid*, trapezius)
Important points:
1. Bend your knees to keep the stress off your back.
2. Keep your back flat. Don't arch or curve it.
3. Your elbows can be slightly bent as you bring the weights out to your sides.
4. Keep your head up and eyes looking forward, not down.
5. Exhale as you lower the weights to the starting position.

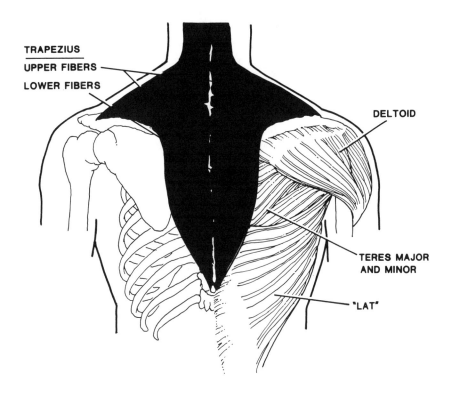

TRAPEZIUS
UPPER FIBERS
LOWER FIBERS

DELTOID

TERES MAJOR
AND MINOR

"LAT"

## Upper Back—Trapezius

Origin—Base of skull, upper sections of the spinal column (vertebrae)
Insertion—collarbone and shoulder blade (scapula)
Fiber Direction—upper fibers diagonal, middle fibers horizontal, lower fibers diagonal
Action—Shrugs shoulders, adducts shoulder blades (scapula), moves them toward the
   midline of the body.

## Exercises for the Trapezius

**Shoulder Shrugs** (develops the *upper fibers* of the trapezius)
Important points:
1. Can be done with a bar, with dumbbells or at a bench press station.
2. Initiate the movement with your shoulders, not your arms. Don't bend them.
3. It is helpful to roll your shoulders either forward or backward.
   The trapezius is involved in the following exercises but not as a primary mover.
Upright Rowing
Behind-the-Head Press
Bent-Over Dumbbell Raise
Lat Pulldown
Seated Row
Bent-Over Row
One Arm Pull-In
Pull-Up

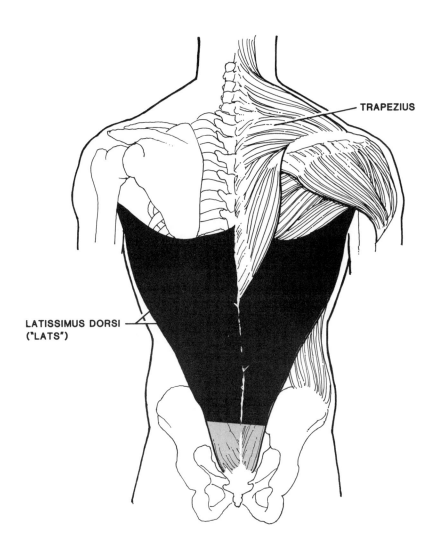

**TRAPEZIUS**

**LATISSIMUS DORSI ("LATS")**

**Mid Back—Latissimus Dorsi ("Lats")**

Origin—middle and lower sections of the spinal column (vertebrae)
Insertion—upper arm
Fiber Direction—diagonal
Action—adduction of the arm, involved whenever the arm is pulled into the body.

## Exercises for the Lats

**Lat Pulldown** (develops the *lats*, trapezius, biceps)
Important points:
1. Use a wide grip and only pull the bar down to the back of your neck.
2. Exhale as you bring the bar up to the starting position.
3. Variations include changing the position of your hands on the bar (narrow grip) and pulling down in front as well as behind you.

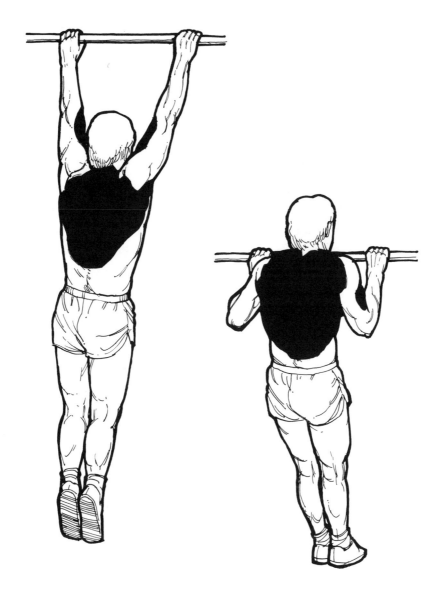

**Pull-Up** (develops the *lats*, trapezius, biceps)
Important points:
1. Come all the way back down to a full hang position for each repetition.
2. Exhale as you come back down to the starting position.
3. For additional resistance, do this exercise with a dumbbell between your legs.
4. Variations include changing your grip from wide to narrow, changing hand position (palms facing you) and bringing your body up in front of the bar.

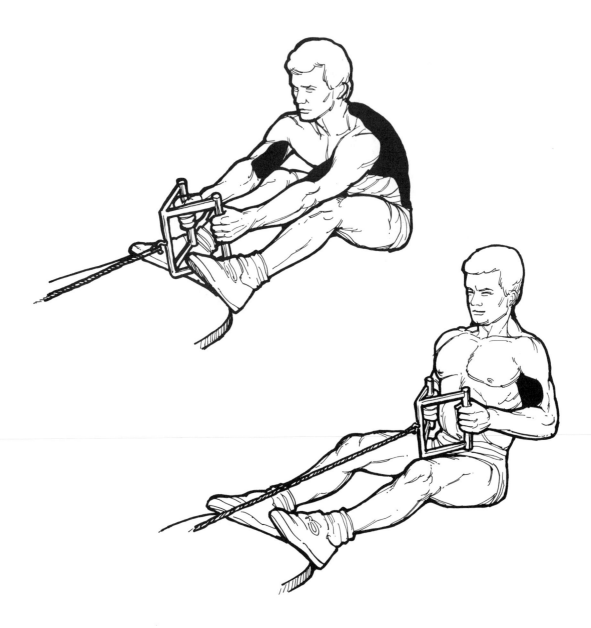

**Seated Rowing** (develops the *lats*, trapezius, biceps)
Important points:
1. Acceptable to bend your knees slightly, but don't use your legs to assist in the pulling.
2. Initiate the action with your arms, not your back.
3. Try to stretch forward to your toes as much as possible.
4. Exhale as you bring the bar back to the starting position.
5. Bring the bar to your stomach (not your chest) with shoulders back.

**One-Arm Dumbbell Pull-In** (develops the *lats*, trapezius, biceps)
Important points:
1. Keep your elbow close to the side of your body.
2. Bring the dumbbell up to your chest.
3. Stretch your arm out as much as possible before starting the lift.
4. Don't roll the other side of your body to assist in movement.
5. Exhale as you lower the dumbbell to the starting position.

**Bent-Over Rowing** (develops the *lats*, trapezius, biceps)
Important points:
1. People with bad backs should avoid this exercise.
2. Make sure you keep your back flat. Don't curve or arch it.
3. Keep your head up and use a wide stance.
4. Bring the bar in to your stomach.
5. Exhale as you lower the weight to the starting position.

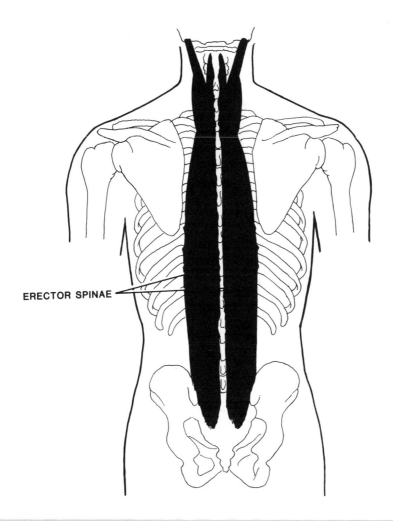

ERECTOR SPINAE

## Lower Back (Erector Spinae)

Origin—Lower spinal column
Insertion—various aspects along spinal column and lower rib cage
Fiber Direction—vertical
Action—Extension of the trunk (arches the back)

### Exercises for the Lower Back

Note: Many of these exercises may be inadvisable for strengthening or rehabilitating the back depending upon your age, sex, genetic predisposition, and past history. Check with a knowledgeable instructor or physical therapist before engaging in any of these exercises. You could be doing more harm than good. Also, Chapter 16 addressed some of these concerns involving the back.

**Back Extensions** (develops the *erector spinae*)
Important points:
1. Come up in a slow, controlled manner to a position parallel to the floor.
2. Do not try to over-arch.
3. This exercise places a lot of stress on the back muscles and spinal column. If your back grows tight or sore from this exercise, discontinue.

**Dead Lift** (develops the *erector spinae*, quadricep, gluteals)
Important points:
1. Use an alternate grip (one palm facing toward you, one away from you).
2. Initiate the action with your legs, then straighten your back as your legs straighten.
3. Roll your shoulders back upon straightening your back.
4. Exhale as you return the weight to the starting position.

**Good Mornings** (develops the *erector spinae*)

Important points:

1. Stance should be shoulder-width or wider.
2. Don't curve your back; keep it straight or flat.
3. Bend over with your legs straight until you feel some tension and return to an upright position.
4. Bend over and come back up in a slow, controlled manner.
5. Exhale as you straighten to the starting position.

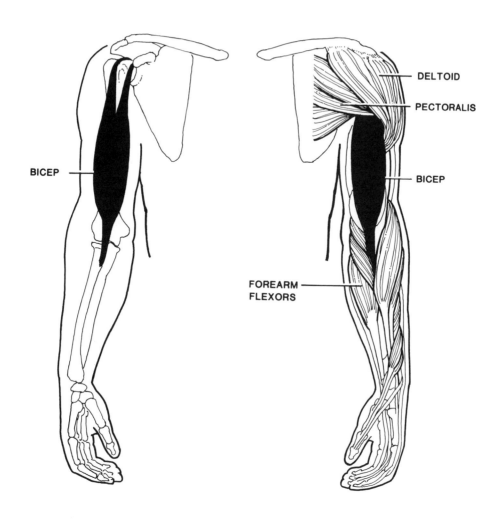

BICEP

DELTOID

PECTORALIS

BICEP

FOREARM
FLEXORS

**Front Part of the Arm—Bicep**
Origin—shoulder
Insertion—forearm
Fiber Direction—vertical
Action—elbow flexion (bends the arm)

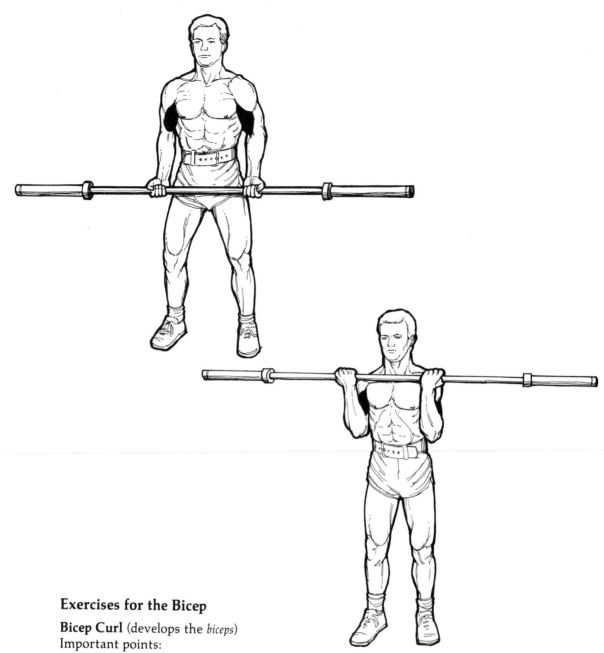

## Exercises for the Bicep

**Bicep Curl** (develops the *biceps*)

Important points:

1. Don't swing the weights. Bring them up and down in a slow, controlled manner.
2. Don't lean back with your upper body to complete the curl.
3. Exhale as you are lowering the weights to the starting position.
4. Variations include different body positions (incline), preacher bench, different pulley systems (high, low), different bars, (free bar, curl bar or dumbbells).

Note: The bicep muscle is involved in many other exercises but not as a primary mover. Curls are the only exercise that isolates the bicep muscle exclusively.

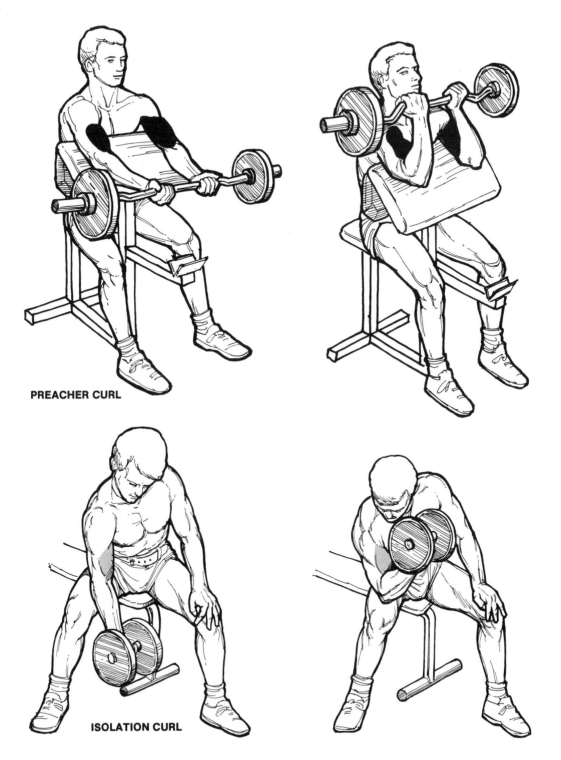

**PREACHER CURL**

**ISOLATION CURL**

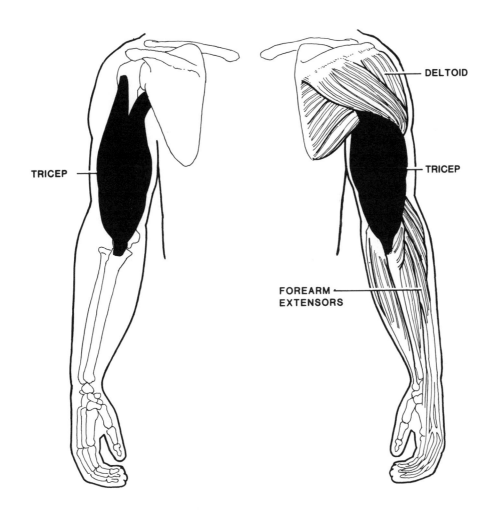

TRICEP

DELTOID

TRICEP

FOREARM
EXTENSORS

**Back Part of the Arm—Tricep**
Origin—upper arm
Insertion—forearm
Fiber Direction—vertical
Action—elbow extension (straightens the arm)

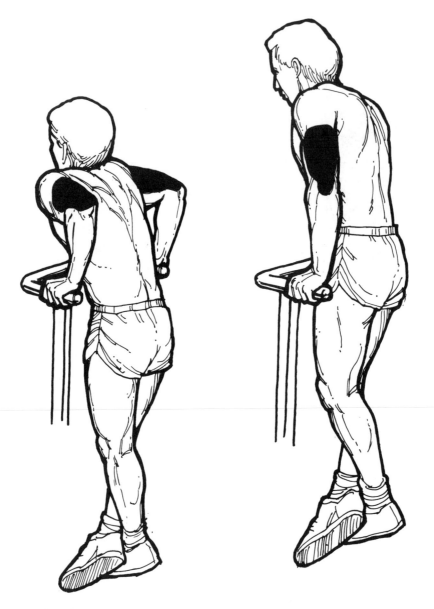

### Exercises for the Tricep

**Dips** (develops the *triceps*, chest)
Important points:
1. Keep your elbows in or straight in line with your hands.
2. Acceptable to do partial dips until you develop the strength to do a full one.
3. Can use dumbbells crossed between your legs for added resistance.
4. Exhale as you push yourself up to the starting position.

**Close-Grip Bench Press** (develops the *tricep*, inside chest, anterior deltoid)
Important points:
1. Grip should be narrower than shoulder-width.
2. Exhale as you push the weight to the starting position.

**Tricep Extension** (high pulley station, develops the *tricep*)

Important points:

1. Keep your elbows close to your body.
2. Don't let your hands come up higher than your chest when returning to the starting position.
3. Extend your arms straight (lock out your elbows).
4. Exhale as you lock or straighten your arms.
5. Variations include using dumbbells and a free bar for extensions as well as different body positions (lying, kneeling, standing).

Note: The tricep is involved in many other exercises but not as a primary mover. The extensions and its variations are the only exercises that isolate the tricep muscle group exclusively.

**DUMBBELL EXTENSION**

**ONE ARM DUMBBELL EXTENSION**

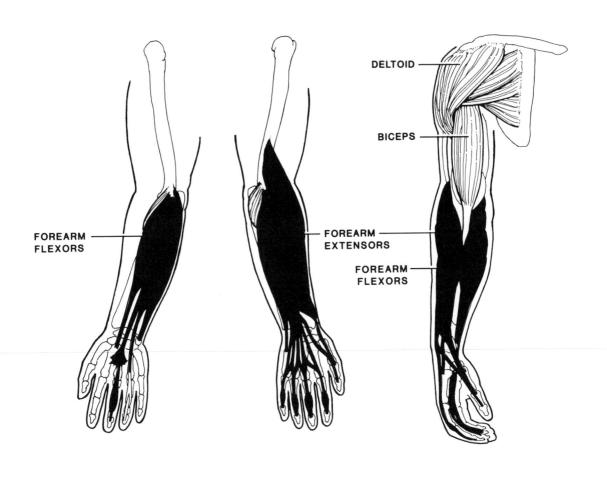

DELTOID

BICEPS

FOREARM
FLEXORS

FOREARM
EXTENSORS

FOREARM
FLEXORS

**Front Part of the Forearm—Wrist Flexors**
Origin—upper arm and forearm
Insertion—below the wrist in the hand
Fiber Direction—vertical
Action—wrist flexion

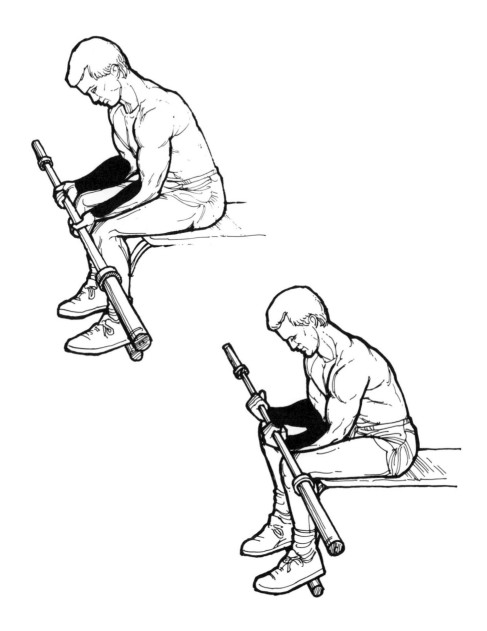

## Exercises for the Wrist

**Wrist Curl** (develops the wrist flexor muscle groups)
Important points:
1. Try to roll your wrists backward and forward as much as possible.
2. This exercise can be done with either a bar or dumbbells.

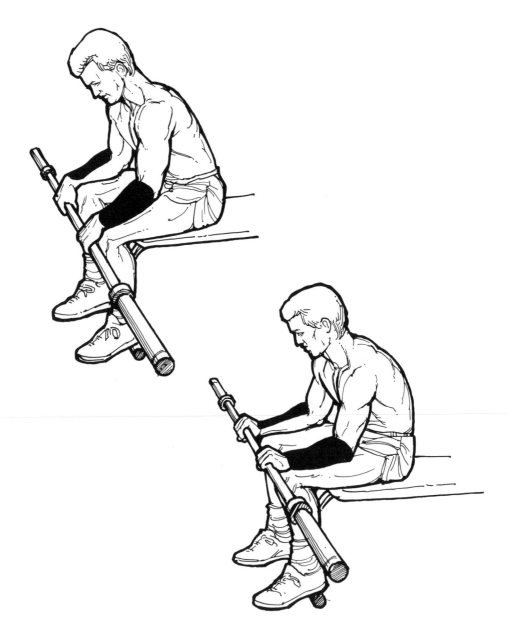

## Back Part of the Forearm—Wrist Extensors

**Wrist Extension** (develops the wrist extensor muscle groups)
Important points:
1. Try to roll your wrists backward and forward as much as possible.
2. This exercise can be done with either a bar or dumbbells.

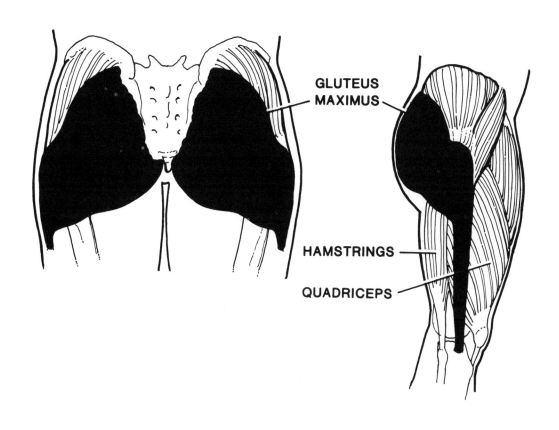

**Buttocks—Gluteus Maximus or "Gluteals"**

Origin—spinal vertebrae and pelvis
Insertion—thigh
Fiber Direction—diagonal
Action—hip extension (moves thigh backward)

## Exercises for the Buttocks

**Lunges** (develops the *quadriceps*, gluteals)
Important points:
1. The longer your step forward, the greater the stress placed on the gluteals.
2. Bend your front knee until your thigh is parallel to the floor.
3. Push back in a straight line, alternate forward leg each repetition.
4. Keep your head up, shoulders back and back flat.
5. Exhale as you push yourself back to the starting position.

**Deep Squat** (develops the *quadricep*, gluteals)
Note: See the description for the squat in the section on quadriceps.

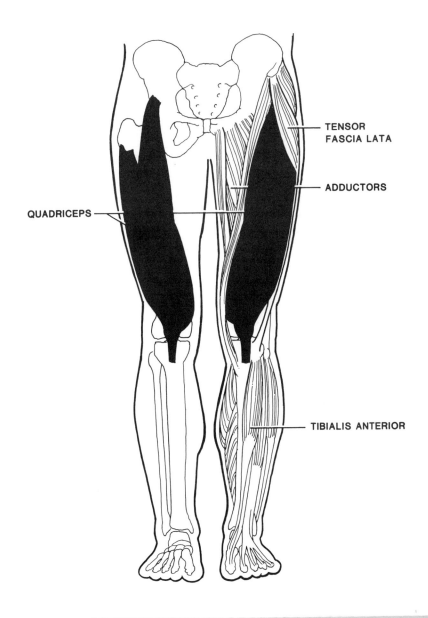

TENSOR
FASCIA LATA

ADDUCTORS

QUADRICEPS

TIBIALIS ANTERIOR

### Front Part of the Thigh—Quadricep

Origin—hip and top part of the thigh
Insertion—patella (knee cap) tendon below the knee
Fiber Direction—vertical
Action—knee extension

## Exercises for the Quadricep

**Squat** (develops the *quadricep*, gluteals)
Important points:
1. Use a wide stance for greater stability.
2. Keep your shoulders back, head up, chest out and back flat.
3. Extremely important not to curve your back when squatting.
4. Exhale as you push and return to the standing position.
5. Can do half-squats until you develop the strength to do a full squat (thighs parallel to the floor).
6. Can develop the gluteals with a deep squat, thighs lower than parallel.

**Knee Extension** (develops the *quadricep*)

Important points:

1. You don't have to straighten your leg all the way. That places a lot of stress on the knee joint.
2. Use a smooth, controlled motion both up and down.
3. Exhale as you straighten your legs.

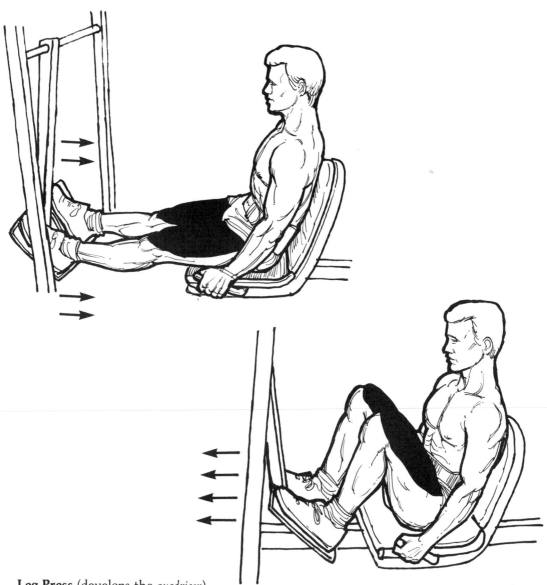

**Leg Press** (develops the *quadricep*)
Important points:
1. Place the balls of your feet on the foot stand.
2. Don't lock out your knees with a lot of force. Straighten your legs slowly.
3. Don't cheat by sitting higher in the chair to get better leverage.
4. Exhale as you extend or straighten your legs.

**Lunges** (develops the *quadricep*, gluteals)
Note: Refer to explanation for buttock exercises.

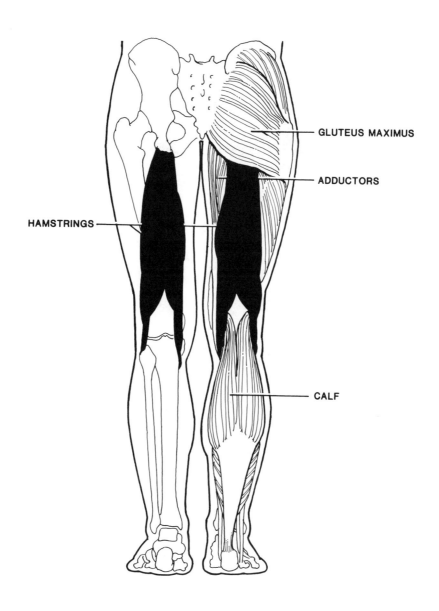

GLUTEUS MAXIMUS

ADDUCTORS

HAMSTRINGS

CALF

**Back Part of the Thigh—Hamstring**

Origin—Pelvis and upper thigh
Insertion—lower leg below the knee
Fiber Direction—vertical
Action—knee flexion

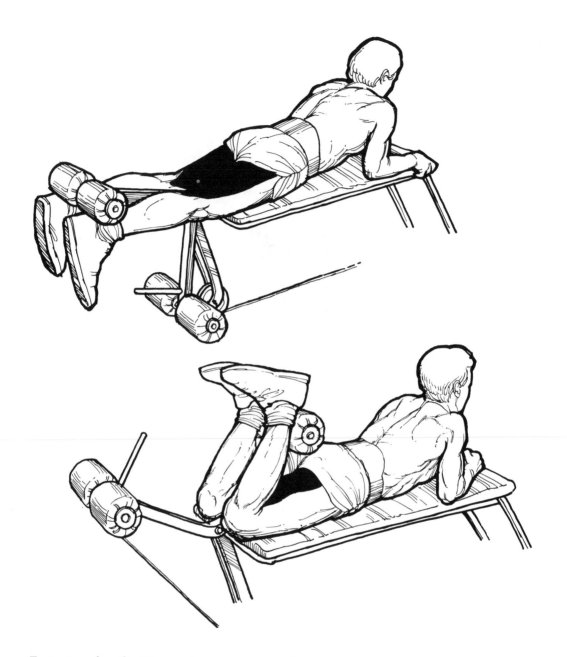

### Exercises for the Hamstring

**Leg Curl** (develops the *hamstring*)
Important points:
1. Try not to arch your back too much when bringing your feet to your buttocks.
2. Exhale as you lower the weight back to the starting position.

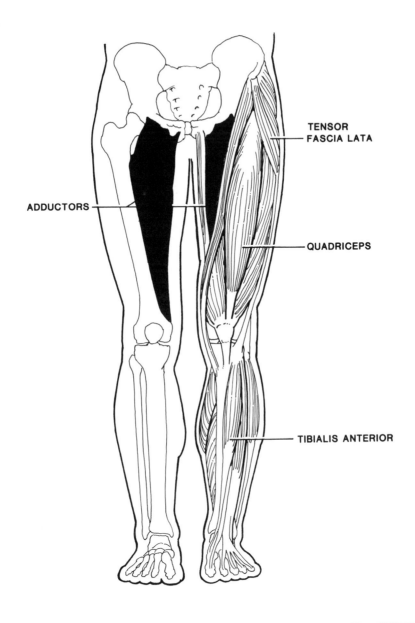

TENSOR
FASCIA LATA

ADDUCTORS

QUADRICEPS

TIBIALIS ANTERIOR

**Inside of the Thigh—Adductors** (several muscle groups)

Origin—Pelvis
Insertion—Inside of thigh on the tibia (bone)
Fiber Direction—Vertical
Action—Adduction of the thigh

## Exercises for the Adductors

**Cross-Over Leg Pull** (develops the *adductors*)
Important points:
1. Keep your knee locked and your leg straight.
2. You don't need to point your toes.
3. Don't pull or lean with your upper body. Use the inside of your thigh only.

**Side-Lying Leg Scissors** (develops the *adductors*)

Important points:

1. Make sure you are lying on your side, not on your back.
2. The higher you hold your outside leg, the greater the stress placed on the adductors.
3. Bring inside leg up in a smooth, controlled manner.

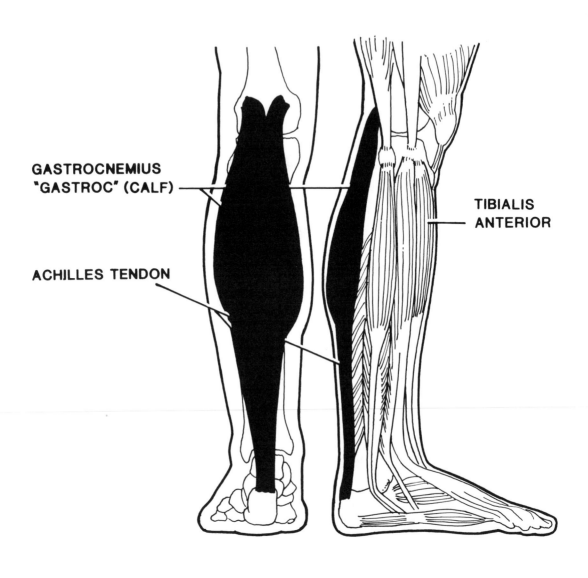

GASTROCNEMIUS
"GASTROC" (CALF)

ACHILLES TENDON

TIBIALIS
ANTERIOR

**Calf—Gastrocnemius ("Gastroc")**

Origin—above knee joint
Insertion—back of the heel
Fiber Direction—vertical
Action—points the toes (plantar flexion of the foot)

## Exercises for the Calf

**Calf Raises** (develops the *gastroc*)
Important points:
1. Try to raise and lower your foot as much as possible.

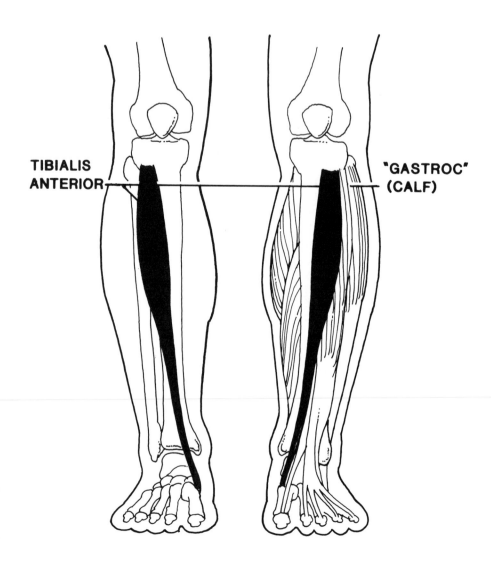

TIBIALIS
ANTERIOR

"GASTROC"
(CALF)

**Front Part of the Calf—Tibialis Anterior**

Origin—front part of the leg below the knee.
Insertion—front part of the foot by the toes.
Fiber Direction—vertical
Action—hooks the toes (dorsal flexion of the foot)

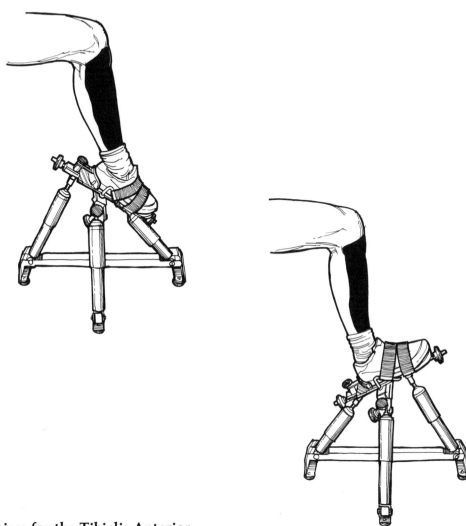

## Exercises for the Tibialis Anterior

**Dorsi-Flexion** (develops the *tibialis anterior*)

Important points:

1. This exercise is good for strengthening the muscle involved in shin splints.
2. This is not a strong muscle group; you will not be able to use much resistance.
3. Try to use a full range of motion both up and down.
4. Variations include having a partner hold your toes as you try to hook them, having a partner hold a towel over your toes while you try to hook them, or using your other foot as resistance and trying to hook your toes against it.

# Appendix

Name _____ Year _____

Age _____ Ht. _____ Wt. _____

*ONE REPETITION MAXIMUM RESULTS*

|  | 1st test | 2nd test | 3rd test |
|---|---|---|---|
| BENCH PRESS |  |  |  |
| SHOULDER PRESS |  |  |  |
| UPRIGHT ROWING |  |  |  |
| LEG PRESS |  |  |  |
| BICEP CURL |  |  |  |
| TRICEP EXTENSION |  |  |  |

*ENDURANCE RESULTS*

| PUSH-UPS |  |  |  |
|---|---|---|---|
| SIT-UPS |  |  |  |
| DIPS |  |  |  |
| PULL-UPS |  |  |  |

## 1-RM INSTRUCTIONS

1. Warm up with a light weight at each lift, completing anywhere from six to 10 repetitions.
2. From that point, you will work your way, by trial and error, to your max.
3. Do not do anymore than one repetition per weight selected as you work toward your max.
4. Record your 1-RM as the highest weight that you successfully lifted.

## ENDURANCE INSTRUCTIONS

1. Using good form and a full ROM, complete as many repetitions as possible. It is permissible to do half, instead of full dips, if you do not have the strength to do a full dip. It is also permissible to do knee push-ups if you cannot do a regular push-up. Pull-ups should be done with your palms facing away from you.

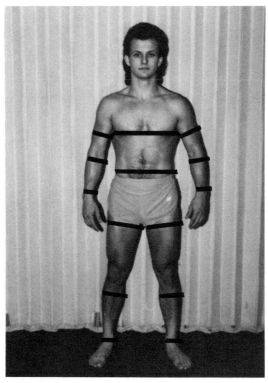

## GIRTH MEASUREMENTS

Note: Girth measurements, although not very scientific, can have a tremendous amount of value to someone trying to either gain or lose weight. It is common for someone lifting weights and trying to lose weight to see very little results on the scale. However, by taking girth measurements, it is possible to document the fact that the person is losing inches (fat) and maintaining muscle tissue. Girth measurement documentation can also indicate where the weight is being lost for someone trying to lose weight. A steel tape is best for these measurements since it eliminates any type of error factor associated with the stretching of cloth or plastic tapes.

WRIST        at the narrowest part.

FOREARM  at the widest part, about three-fourths of the way up from the wrist.

ARM          halfway between the elbow and shoulder in a relaxed position.

CHEST        across the lower part of the chest.

WAIST        across the belly button.

THIGH        upper thigh just underneath the buttocks.

CALF          at the widest part, about three-fourths of the way up from the ankle.

ANKLE        at the narrowest point just above the ankle bones.

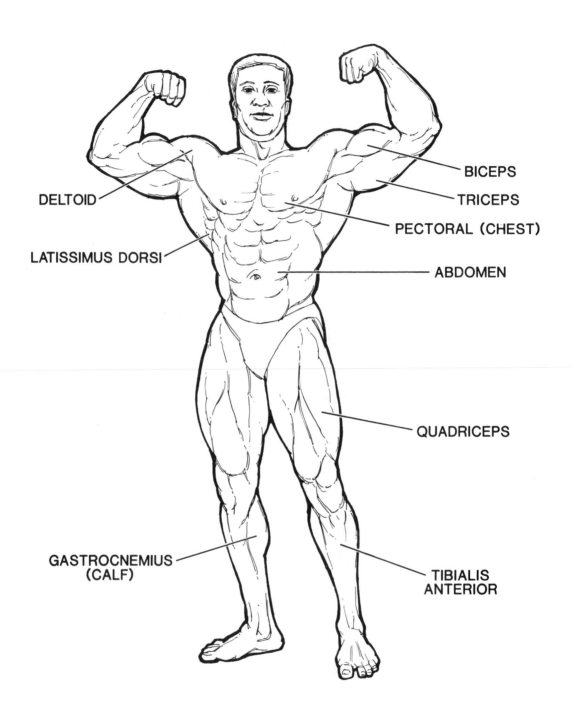

DELTOID

BICEPS

TRICEPS

PECTORAL (CHEST)

LATISSIMUS DORSI

ABDOMEN

QUADRICEPS

GASTROCNEMIUS
(CALF)

TIBIALIS
ANTERIOR

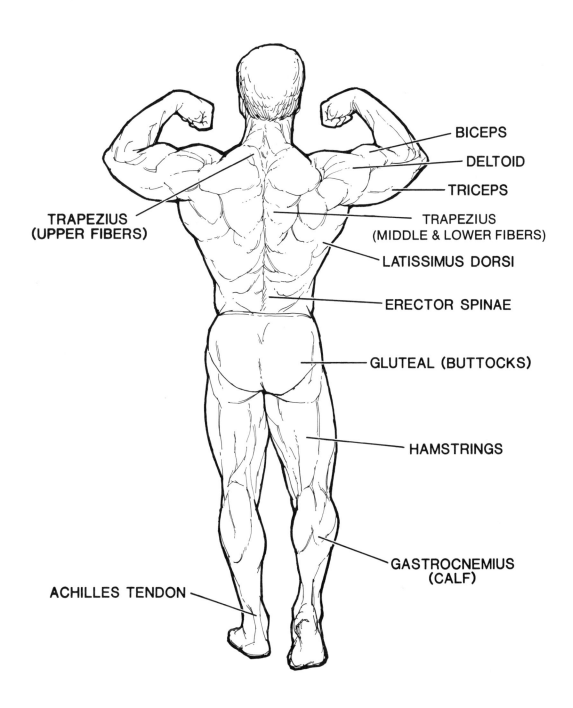

BICEPS

DELTOID

TRICEPS

TRAPEZIUS
(MIDDLE & LOWER FIBERS)

LATISSIMUS DORSI

ERECTOR SPINAE

GLUTEAL (BUTTOCKS)

HAMSTRINGS

GASTROCNEMIUS
(CALF)

TRAPEZIUS
(UPPER FIBERS)

ACHILLES TENDON

# WEIGHT TRAINING CHART

Name _____  Age _____  Height _____  Weight _____

| | Date: | | | Date: | | | Date: | | | Date: | | | Date: | | | Date: | | |
|---|---|---|---|---|---|---|---|---|---|---|---|---|---|---|---|---|---|---|
| CHEST | LBS | REP | SET | LBS | REP | SET | LBS | REP | SET | LBS | REP | SET | LBS | REP | SET | LBS | REP | SET |
| Bench Press | | | | | | | | | | | | | | | | | | |
| Incline Dumbell Press | | | | | | | | | | | | | | | | | | |
| Dumbell Pullover | | | | | | | | | | | | | | | | | | |
| Cable Crossover | | | | | | | | | | | | | | | | | | |
| Flat-Bench Flies | | | | | | | | | | | | | | | | | | |

| | Date: | | | Date: | | | Date: | | | Date: | | | Date: | | | Date: | | |
|---|---|---|---|---|---|---|---|---|---|---|---|---|---|---|---|---|---|---|
| TRICEPS | LBS | REP | SET | LBS | REP | SET | LBS | REP | SET | LBS | REP | SET | LBS | REP | SET | LBS | REP | SET |
| Pulley Push-Down | | | | | | | | | | | | | | | | | | |
| Dumbell Tricep Extension | | | | | | | | | | | | | | | | | | |
| Lying Overhead Extension | | | | | | | | | | | | | | | | | | |
| Dumbell Kickbacks | | | | | | | | | | | | | | | | | | |
| Pulley Tricep Extension | | | | | | | | | | | | | | | | | | |

| | Date: | | | Date: | | | Date: | | | Date: | | | Date: | | | Date: | | |
|---|---|---|---|---|---|---|---|---|---|---|---|---|---|---|---|---|---|---|
| BACK | LBS | REP | SET | LBS | REP | SET | LBS | REP | SET | LBS | REP | SET | LBS | REP | SET | LBS | REP | SET |
| Lat Pulldown | | | | | | | | | | | | | | | | | | |
| Seated Bent Rows | | | | | | | | | | | | | | | | | | |
| Dumbell Bent Rows | | | | | | | | | | | | | | | | | | |
| Hyperextension | | | | | | | | | | | | | | | | | | |

## SHOULDERS

| Exercise | Date: LBS | REP | SET | Date: LBS | REP | SET | Date: LBS | REP | SET | Date: LBS | REP | SET |
|---|---|---|---|---|---|---|---|---|---|---|---|---|
| Military Press | | | | | | | | | | | | |
| Shoulder Shrugs | | | | | | | | | | | | |
| Barbell Upright Row | | | | | | | | | | | | |
| Dumbell Side Laterals | | | | | | | | | | | | |
| Cable Crossover | | | | | | | | | | | | |
| Front Horizontal Raise | | | | | | | | | | | | |

## BICEPS

| Exercise | Date: LBS | REP | SET | Date: LBS | REP | SET | Date: LBS | REP | SET | Date: LBS | REP | SET |
|---|---|---|---|---|---|---|---|---|---|---|---|---|
| Barbell Curls | | | | | | | | | | | | |
| Preacher Curls | | | | | | | | | | | | |
| Alternating Dumbell Curls | | | | | | | | | | | | |
| Incline Dumbell Curls | | | | | | | | | | | | |
| Concentration Curls | | | | | | | | | | | | |

## LEGS

| Exercise | Date: LBS | REP | SET | Date: LBS | REP | SET | Date: LBS | REP | SET | Date: LBS | REP | SET |
|---|---|---|---|---|---|---|---|---|---|---|---|---|
| Leg Press | | | | | | | | | | | | |
| Cable Crossover Abduction | | | | | | | | | | | | |
| Cable Crossover Abduction | | | | | | | | | | | | |
| Leg Lunges | | | | | | | | | | | | |
| Leg Curls | | | | | | | | | | | | |
| Calf-Raises | | | | | | | | | | | | |

# Index